WIN*ology*
World-Class Performance
by Joel Scrivner

Published by Blaze Publishing House
BlazePublishingHouse.com

This book or parts thereof may not be reproduced in part or in whole, in any form, stored in a retrieval system, or transmitted in any form by any means—electronic, mechanical, photocopy, recording, or otherwise—without prior written permission of the publisher, except as provided by United States of America copyright law.

Manuscript Development - Kent Booth
Editors - Laura-Lee Booth & Billy Kingham
Pagination, Interior Design, and Layout - Laura-Lee Booth
Prepared for Publication - Ministry Solutions, LLC
Cover Design - Steve John (www.thesmartcreativesolution.com)
Photograph on Back Cover - Alisa Albers

ISBN-13: 978-0-9968803-1-2
Copyright © 2015 by Joel Scrivner
All rights reserved.

WHAT PEOPLE ARE SAYING ABOUT WIN*OLOGY* AND JOEL SCRIVNER

"Within the pages of WIN*ology* is a simple, yet challenging blueprint that will help us to move towards excellence in every area of our lives. And who better to lead us by the hand and take us through this than Joel Scrivner, who has walked these principles out through testing and trial, victory and triumph in his own life. WIN*ology* works! I've witnessed it first-hand."

David Hollie, Store Team Leader
Whole Foods Market

"A true winner, Joel Scrivner is a living testimony to the system he has created. WIN*ology* is a strategic system that is sure to elevate your personal life, leadership team, or entire business. This book will challenge, enlighten, and inspire the best in anyone who reads it."

Erin Botsford
Founder & CEO Botsford Financial Group
Top 100 Women Financial Advisors

"The principles Joel Scrivner shares in WIN*ology* can help anyone turn their dream into a reality. We have used these methods for winning to build our recipe and travel website from a hobby into a thriving family business that allows both my husband and I to work together from home and provides opportunities to travel all over the world as a family. I would recommend WIN*ology* to anyone who needs encouragement and know-how to take their talents and plans to the next level. Success is possible, and WIN*ology* offers the kick in the pants needed to set you on your way!"

Sommer Collier
Founder & CEO
A Spicy Perspective (ASpicyPerspective.com)

"WIN*ology* lays out the blueprint that every organization and individual can follow for success. From defining what it takes to win to initiating lasting change, this book will challenge you to go higher than you ever thought possible. Joel does more than define a strategy to win; he shows you how."

Ryan Binkley, President
Generational Equity
M&A Advisor - Valuation Firm of the Year 2014

"WIN*ology* is sensational! Joel lays out revolutionary and breakthrough strategies that when applied, will ensure you reach new plateaus in life. For anyone who desires to achieve greatness in any area; WIN*ology* is a must read!"

Charles Beauford, Founder & CEO
BeauMed Consultants & MedEdge BPM
Former VP of Sales & Business Development of
StatScript Biologicals

"WIN*ology* is a goldmine! I couldn't put this book down! Joel has brilliantly laid out the principles that every winner has in common. I will personally read this book again and again!"

Kevin Boyd
Founder & CEO
K&G Enterprises

"If you are looking for a competitive edge in life to be a true winner, then this book is for you! Joel Scrivner has created an exceptional success system called WIN*ology* that will show you the steps necessary to be successful in both your personal and professional life. We all have the ability to WIN in life; and with Joel's help, you will achieve extraordinary results by following a few simple steps. I highly recommend you read this book and to do it NOW!"

Michelle Prince
Zig Ziglar Motivational Speaker
Best-Selling Author & Self-Publishing Expert

"Joel brings to bear a fresh approach to moving past failure—a framework of four phases and nine critical steps—borne of his personal failures and successes, and with terrific examples of people we know. Engaging, challenging, and genuine—a great read! This can be done, and Joel is providing a new way to behave and think about WINNING!"

Salman Mistry
Mistry Capital & Co.

"Joel Scrivner truly understands the science of winning. He is a true champion and a master teacher. WIN*ology* is a must-read for everyone that desires to WIN in everything they do."

Danny Bae, Entrepreneur, Motivational Speaker,
& Leadership Development Teacher
VP of Sales for ACN

"This is a different book. Joel has written WIN*ology* for those working in uncharted territory who have taken a leap of faith with little else to go on except a firm belief in themselves. Joel has decoded the secrets of winning. If you are going after something considered impossible to achieve, the wisdom you pick up from Joel will not just make you a winner, it will turn you into the rarest of bright shining stars."

James Mathews, Founder
ElevateX
Chairman of Health 2.0 India
Director of Indian School of Business
Jr. NBA & FIBA Certified Coach
Mentor at University of California, Berkeley, & Ashoka University

"Joel Scrivner is one of life's wonderfully rare winners who doesn't hesitate to share those secret things he has learned with the world. Although on the surface this might appear to be yet another successful person cashing in on the 'self-help book craze,' understand that Joel has been refining this message, sharing it for years. I first met Joel over ten years ago and watched as he convinced thousands of young people that they could become—and, in fact, already were—legendary. I've watched as he's worked with thousands of individuals, business people, and families convincing them that they, too, were champions. And finally, I watched him live this concept out while walking through personal defeats and painful tragedies, never hiding from them, but instead incorporating them into the life of a champion. By helping us understand that winning is not some ethereal lottery but actually a science which can be studied, embraced, and conquered, Joel has provided valuable tools to change lives and destinies."

Kevin Brown, President & CEO
IPC, LLC
Founder, The Maroon Institute Learning Culture
Founder, The Greater Truth

"After coaching hundreds of executive leaders and teaching in business school, I am now more convinced than ever that our modern-day notion of greatness is a sham. The "born with it" philosophy is rooted in the fatalistic excuse of apathy, that countless world-class performers have proven entirely wrong. The one overarching prerequisite to winning and becoming the 1% of top performers is the willingness to do what others will simply not do. This is the inescapable reality of greatness. WIN*ology* has finally conceptualized this in a systemized way that makes the notion not only appealing, but possible. To the victor goes the spoils."

Dr. Brian Epperson
CEO & Founder Human Performance Advisors
Dean, Chesapeake Energy School of Business
Oklahoma Wesleyan University

"As a former collegiate and professional athlete, now Fortune 75 company executive, I've had my share of winning experiences. These winning experiences came with a lot of trial and error. If you're like me, experiencing wins here and there in life, business, and relationships is not good enough. You want to win on a consistent basis and in every area of your life. That's why when it comes to winning you need to learn from the best, someone who has competed and won at the highest levels of competition. Every Sunday I have the distinct pleasure to listen and learn from such a person, Joel Scrivner. A former world-class martial arts champion, successful business leader, and now leading thousands in life as a pastor, Joel, knows about winning. Joel's leadership in my life extends much further than a pastoral relationship. He challenges me to approach every business transaction as if I've already won. His messages inspire, motivate, and encourage me to be the best I can be in that moment. I encourage every leader to read WINology. This book will provide you with key takeaways in becoming the best leader you can be."

James Wheeler
Vice President, Commercial Property Insurance
Fortune 75 Corporate Executive

"Joel will be proclaimed as the best 21st century success coach in America. His book, WINology, is a masterpiece; a road map for success in life and business. As a writer of 62 books, I would never expect a new author to write such a dynamic book. But Joel has. I 100% recommend it."

Mike Evans
#1 New York Times Best-Selling Author

Acknowledgments

To my parents, Ken and Jean Scrivner, for instilling in me all the ingredients for success.

To my wife, Jennifer, for lovingly believing in me and sticking with me through thick and thin for two decades... and counting.

To my daughters, Sydney and Blakely, for always seeing, speaking and inspiring the best in their Daddy. I will not let you down.

To my pastors, Mike and Kathy Hayes, for inspiring me to dream increasingly bigger.

To my friends: James Mathews, David Hollie, Charles Beauford, Mike Connaway, Brian Epperson, Stephen Hayes and Dan Collier for provoking me to act on this idea.

To my instructors: Jack Bell, Jim Hammons, Rob Ellis, and Scott McNeely for pushing me beyond myself.

To my friend and publisher, Kent Booth, for "making it do what it do, baby!"

To my father, Ken, and friends, Suzanne Holland and Laura-Lee Booth, for polishing and proofing the project. I am forever grateful.

Contents

Foreword by Lance Wallnau		13
1	The Winner Within	15
2	The Science of Winning	21
3	Step 1: Urgent Excellence	37
4	Step 2: Positive Conviction	53
5	Step 3: Decisive Action	73
6	Step 4: Master Your Craft	89
7	Step 5: Playing Inbounds	105
8	Step 6: Tenacious Endurance	121
9	Step 7: Strategic Partnership	141
10	Step 8: Contagious Kindness	159
11	Step 9: Great Love	175

Foreword

Joel has already lived a multi-faceted life, putting his research to work successfully as a world-class martial artist and in his inspiring work building a successful non-profit organization. Like his life, Joel's WIN*ology* methodology is broad enough to include almost any field yet specific enough to demand a commitment out of someone seeking to follow it. This is a perfect guide for anyone who is frustrated by desires and visions they cannot seem to materialize. Consider this quote from Joel:

> "There's nothing wrong with dreaming, as long as you wake up from your dreams and put action to them! Without practical application and Decisive Action regarding your positive belief system, your dreams will only remain fantasies and fairy tales. Beliefs and a Positive Conviction are desperately needed, but belief—no matter how positive it may be—without action is dead and worthless."

Practical application is often what is lacking in books, but Joel furnishes this in abundance, along with a wide range of incisive, contemporary and historic examples. This book is an entertaining, fast-paced, and informative reading experience. Sugar Ray Robinson has a quote Joel relates:

> *"To be a champ you have to believe in yourself when nobody else will."*

This book and Joel will help you believe in *you*. Follow this WIN*ology* formula and it won't be long before we will be reading *your* books and celebrating *your* victories. Nothing would make Joel happier.

Dr. Lance Wallnau, CEO/Founder
Lance Learning Group

1

The Winner Within

The year, 1987. The place, Tulsa, OK. Even though I was only the ripe age of 14 at the time, I was about to learn an incredibly valuable lesson—one that would set the course for the remainder of my life.

As a sprouting ninth grader, I had already accomplished more in the art of Taekwondo than most people do in a lifetime. Within three years, I had earned my black belt and had been crowned the U.S. Taekwondo national champion in my federation. Each month I was competing in local, state, or regional tournaments, stacking up first place trophies and medals left and right. My performance on the mat was reaching the top of my game; however, not everything in my life was clicking on all cylinders.

While the world of Taekwondo was seemingly at my fingertips, I found myself struggling with a handful of school subjects, namely Freshman Spanish I. Even with a bedroom full of trophies and medals, bringing home a "D" in my first semester of Spanish left me with this sinking feeling: a sit-down conversation with my father, Ken, was ensuing.

I was right.

During my anticipated father-to-son chat, Dad posed a thought-provoking question: "Joel, why can't you take the same effort, discipline, and excellence that you exude in your martial arts training and apply it to Spanish?" My 14 year-old, hyper-testosteronal response was instant and simple: "Because, Dad, Spanish is boring and fighting is fun." Not satisfied with the answer, my dad probed deeper.

"Is everything about the martial arts fun? I mean, the thousands of push-ups, the endless stretching, and countless hours of excruciating workouts—not to mention the bloody noses and black eyes. Is it all fun? Certainly, you don't like all of those parts, do you?"

Pops had me.

When it came down to it, what I loved about the martial arts was *winning*. Actually, I was addicted to winning. My passion and daily discipline to win drove me to spend hours of practice and tedious training, often pushing through physical pain. I was determined to be the guy at the end of the match standing on the winner's platform, with his hand raised in victory, and a medal around his neck. That was me—and my dad knew it.

As if his first two questions weren't enough, Dad saved the dagger, which pierced my heart, for last: "Why can't you do the things you don't want to do and don't like to do in order to accomplish the goal of getting an "A" in Spanish? Isn't getting an "A" fun? Wouldn't you consider that *winning* in Spanish?"

Challenge accepted.

Over the next few months, I set out to prove (mainly to myself) that the same effort it took to be a martial arts champion could be translated into another area—Spanish.

> **... Winning is a science.**

By the end of the next semester that "D" came up to an "A," and I've never looked back. A switch had flipped in my brain. From that moment on, school was a breeze and I knew anything was possible. But it was more than a way to get good grades. Something far greater happened in me. For the first time in my life, I realized that winning wasn't some magical potion and didn't happen "just because." No, winning is a science.

Thus, the concept of WIN*ology* was birthed.

- WELCOME TO WINNING -

Little did I know how a simple conversation with my life's hero would turn out to be the driving force of success in every area of my life. It would shape every facet of my being including my relationships, my belief system, my self-expectations, and my future. Some years later, by following and pursuing the science and disciplines of winning, I won my first Global Taekwondo Federation World Championship. I went on to win three more world championship gold medals and then built a thriving martial arts business in the years to follow. But that was only the beginning.

The lessons I've learned and developed have helped me flourish in every facet of life. Those secrets, methods, and disciplines I used while training myself, along with thousands of others, over the past 25 years are now compiled into this system, WIN*ology*. It's my honor to share them with you now.

What exactly is WIN*ology*? It's a systematic program, designed through the lens of a world-class competitor, to give you the competitive edge necessary to fight through any challenge and rise to the top in any field you desire. Through decades of scientific process—including inquiry, research, hypothesis, experimentation, and conclusion—WIN*ology* has been designed to challenge, push, and compel you to believe and become a new version of yourself.

Understand, WIN*ology* isn't about the obnoxious, selfish, corporate brown-nose ladder climbing that's so prevalent in our age. No, it's a system that will train you to outperform those around you to such a degree that you become the most obvious choice for raises, promotions, contracts, or capital infusions.

You're embarking on a journey into yourself—to discover and unleash the winner that's already inside you. It matters not your gender, age, whether you're fresh out of high school or decades into a successful career. This step-by-step system will teach you how to think, speak, and act like the winner you were born to be. By adhering to this system, you'll begin to win in life at an entirely different level, and achieve unparalleled happiness and success.

Don't shortchange yourself by thinking this system is only for people in business (though it *can* and *will* radically transform you and your business). WIN*ology* is equally as powerful for the stay-at-home mom as it is for the corporate attorney looking to become a partner of the firm. Regardless of past successes or failures, winning at whatever you choose is about to become *your new way of life!*

WIN*ology* is a system that works. I'm living proof, and there are countless numbers of others—some you will meet in later chapters—who have also lived by this system with astonishing results. I know it will change your life, as well.

The winner inside you is about to be unleashed. Let me be the first to say:

"Welcome to the New You!"

2

THE SCIENCE OF WINNING

If you're anything like me, the very sight of the word "science" may give you nightmares of grueling college courses like anatomy and physiology, or organic and inorganic chemistry! Let me assure you, that's not the case for this book. I promise you the word "science," even though a bit intimidating and sometimes overwhelming at first, will take on a whole new meaning by the end of this chapter.

Previously, I mentioned how part of my discovery was coming to the realization that winning is a science. Now, what exactly does that mean? And, how did I figure it out? This chapter concludes with my personal discovery and journey of this illumination, but let's get to first things first by defining "science"—and it won't be boring or intimidating.

The Oxford Dictionary defines "science" this way:[1]

The intellectual and practical activity encompassing

the systematic study of the structure and behavior of the physical and natural world through observation and experimentation.

While that's probably more adjectives than you bargained for, I like to define "science" as:

The study of a matter to learn the inner workings, potential, and projected future of said matter.

With this in mind, how does The Science of Winning operate? Simple. It functions just like the science of any other subject.

- The Evolution of a Winner -

Even though winning seems to be an elusive and intangible concept—taking on many forms in essentially every field and arena of life—this reality is actually what makes it so scientific. There's not a single field in which the strategies, tactics, and techniques of a winner cannot be studied. Whether running, dancing, writing, selling, acting, or becoming champions in personal relationships, the "greats" in any field don't become great on their own. They learn the secret of winning, which is really no secret at all.

Modern aviation is a perfect example. From the beginning of mankind, man has been fascinated with flight. The idea that man could defy gravity and fly like a bird has always been both enthralling and scientific. Those who made great gains, breakthroughs, and accomplishments—

people like Leonardo da Vinci, the Wright Brothers, or Howard Hughes—would all be classified as winners in aviation. How did they achieve such great feats? It's quite simple: They submitted themselves to the four phases of *The Evolution of a Winner*.

> **Imitation is an inarguable initial step of every artistic phenom.**

Understanding and adhering to these same four phases will propel you forward from your current status and position toward world-class performance.

- PHASE 1: IMITATION -

Imitation is the first form of scientific discovery. It's the "How did they do that?" phase. Every scientific process begins with an inquiry. Basic curiosity and intrigue are the catalysts for becoming a winner. Once you come to know how predecessors accomplished the incredible, you can then move to the point of replicating it yourself. But first, you must have an understanding of how it was previously accomplished.

Has *Imitation* ever succeeded? Well, you decide for yourself. Pablo Picasso was inspired by and imitated Vincent Van Gogh, who studied and copied Claude Monet, who was influenced by and replicated Rembrandt, who admired and initially imitated Michelangelo. Each of these legendary artists were inspired and influenced by their predecessors. This evidence is clearly obvious in the progression of their individual works. *Imitation* is an inarguable initial step of every artistic phenom.

But let's bring it up to our day and age. The legendary comedian, Jim Carey, started his journey by studying and mimicking one of "the greats," Steve Martin. Today, Jim Carey still carries many of Martin's signature traits long after developing his own unique comedic style. Oprah Winfrey stated that she began practicing her public speaking in her childhood by imitating her pastor and orating memorized portions of scripture. This child preacher prodigy went on to evolve into the "Queen of Daytime TV." International pop music star, Bruno Mars, locked himself away as a teen and studied the godfather of soul, James Brown. (If you don't believe it, just watch Bruno in concert!) Featured in the 2015 smash hit, "Uptown Funk," Bruno boldly croons he's so hot that he's "Gotta' kiss myself, I'm so pretty."[2] It just doesn't get much more "James Brown" than that!

Winning can be studied, tested, and dissected, but even more exciting is the fact that it can then be duplicated.

Imitation is the first action step of The Evolution of a Winner. It always has been. From our infancy, we instinctively watch and imitate. It's how we initially learn anything and everything. So, how can The Science of Winning apply to your vocation, hobbies, or relationships? It's simple. Look at the "great ones" in any desired field or skill set, and study what they did and do. Inquire, hypothesize, experiment. Winning can be studied, tested, and dissected, but even more exciting is the fact that it can then be duplicated. *Imitation* of the "great ones" is the genesis of becoming great yourself. You're on your way.

- PHASE 2: INNOVATION -

After the phase of *Imitation* is perfected, you then begin to morph into a new form: from scientist to artist. No longer are you only replicating; now you're creating. This is where you begin to use your own imagination and expanding ability, moving beyond mastering the techniques and practices of your predecessors and into your own innovation and improvisation. Your expertise of the matter begins to release an artistic expression in which you devise better ways to accomplish more than those you previously admired. Like Michelangelo and the Sistine Chapel, the artist (you) raises and illuminates a beautiful new ceiling.

Let's return to the aeronautical example for a moment. Who was the first person in history to study flight? No one really knows. What we do know is how each person imitated and then innovated along the way. Finally, in December 1903, Orville and Wilbur Wright launched a new artistic design—a system of flight—that broke through all of their predecessors' failed attempts.

The Wright Brothers would be the first to penetrate the barrier of human flight, but it was just the initial breakthrough.

Many other accomplishments would soon follow as fellow pioneers like Alexander Graham Bell, Armand and Henri Dufaux, and Amelia Earhart had their day in the sun. Modern-day aeronautical scientists have now become "aeronautical artists," designing beautiful creations which defy gravity and inspire dreams. These scientific artists continue to innovate in the world of aviation, melding technology and design into an art form that the visionary pioneers could only have dreamed of.

We've seen the same type of metamorphosis in the area of personal computers over the past 30 years. In a field once predominately occupied by coders and programmers, we've watched *Imitation* turn to *Innovation* right before our very eyes. The power of processing that used to require a room full of computers, we now hold in our hands. (Thank you, Steve Jobs.) What would the world of computer science be without the progression of innovative artists?

The same can be true for you in your respective field. As you move from scientist to artist, you will begin to innovate beyond the accomplishments of those you previously revered. Yes, you will still admire their work and artistry but in a different light. Their victories and winning status once inspired you to dream and gave you hope and a purpose. Now, your victory is their victory. But even greater than you becoming a winner at this moment is how your victory will fuel the fire of those yet to come.

– Phase 3: Inspiration –

Winning is a state of mind. The *Inspiration* phase is when you transition from research and expression into a place of transcendence. No longer are you moved by what you merely see and hear; now you feel and know things to which others are oblivious. You might not even cognitively recognize this distinction, mainly because you now see the world differently than others.

In this stage, winning in your field is no longer just what you study, replicate, or reinvent; winning is your new state of mind. Does it sound too far-fetched? It's not. Not only is this mindset obtainable, it's well within your reach.

While there are countless numbers of real life examples for this particular scenario, let's use basketball legend, Michael Jordan.

Arguably one of the greatest (if not *the* greatest) basketball players of all time, Michael Jordan didn't begin his illustrious career in the Hall of Fame. In fact, it was just the opposite. Jordan started the game of basketball just like every other kid, admiring his old school NBA heroes and imitating their techniques. He wasn't always the "great one." The first time he tried out for his North Carolina high school varsity squad, he didn't even make it. As a sophomore standing five-feet-eleven-inches, Jordan was deemed too short for the varsity team. So, what did he do? He hit the gym. It was time for *Innovation*.

For the next entire year, Michael Jordan rigorously

trained while playing on the junior varsity team. His efforts to improve his game—combined with a fortuitous four-inch growth spurt the following summer—landed him a spot on the varsity team the very next season. Jordan was now a winner in the area of high school basketball, but he was just getting started.

> **When winning becomes your life's identity, everything changes.**

In his quest to continue building, strengthening, and developing his game, Michael attended the nationally renowned Five-Star Basketball Camp during the summer before his senior year. It was at this camp where he met the University of North Carolina's legendary head basketball coach, Dean Smith. Later that year, Jordan signed a letter of intent to attend UNC on a full-ride basketball scholarship. He would go on to play three years for the Tar Heels, winning an NCAA basketball national championship along with the prestigious "College Player of the Year" award.

But his quest for greatness continued.

In 1984, the Chicago Bulls selected Michael Jordan as their third overall pick in the NBA draft, but they didn't plan to keep him! Their original intent was to trade him for someone bigger—a move which would now be considered preposterous. No matter how loud the critics yelled, Michael Jordan never ceased to improve his game, leading the Chicago Bulls to six NBA world championships. From *Imitation* to *Innovation* to *Inspiration*, Michael Jordan transcended conventional thinking.

Winning became his state of mind.

True, you might not be an NBA megastar in the making, but this same path of winning is possible for you. You can move from the scientific study of others who have obtained championship status in your field to mastering your own artistic expression, wherein the world becomes your canvas. At that point, you begin to approach every situation, scenario, and opposition from the wisdom of your past victories. You're no longer intimidated by challenges and opposition but rather invigorated and even more, inspired!

At this phase, you've witnessed yourself winning so much that it's now your default state of mind.

Winning is your new way of thinking.

Winning is what you expect.

The possibilities are now endless. Moving from *Imitation* and *Innovation* to *Inspiration* releases your limitless creativity. Your confidence is in full stride. You've found your "mojo!" What takes others weeks, months, and even years to accomplish, you complete in a matter of minutes, hours, or days. You've mastered your craft to the point where it's become part of your being.

Now it's time to transform into the final phase of *The Evolution of Winning*—the phase which positions you for greatness in your field.

- Phase 4: Identification -

When winning becomes your life's identity, everything changes. You begin to approach every situation with the expectation of winning, not just the possibility of victory. Even temporary setbacks or momentary losses aren't ultimate defeats, but rather opportunities to reset the scientific process. Now, you begin to view "failure" through the eyes of the great Henry Ford. He described failure this way:

> *"Failure is simply the opportunity to begin again, this time more intelligently."*

In the face of seeming defeat, the winner's internal dialog is, "What can I learn here?" "How did I end up in this place?" "What steps can I take to assure I won't be here again?" Losing is no longer a part of your long-term destiny. Why? Because you're a winner. Winning is what you do. Winning is who you are. No longer a mere survivor, you're now a "thriver." There's no room for doubt. Failure is never an acceptable destination. In fact, any and all fears of failing become the fuel that propels you to victory.

To those who never obtain this level of success, these thought processes and attitudes can sound ultra-cocky and arrogant. That's simply not the case. Confidence in one's capabilities is essentially the winner's next-level state of mind and mental frame of reference. In essence, how you see yourself projects how you perform, and how you influence those around you.

When winning becomes your identity, it's evident to all. Wherever you go in your sphere of expertise, everyone identifies you as a winner. They actually expect you to win. Why? Because winning is more than just a shot-in-the-dark fallacy; winning is your scientifically-proven, artistically-enhanced, inspired identity . . . and everybody knows it. Just ask the poor guys given the daunting task of guarding Michael Jordan in his prime.

They all knew Jordan was a winner.

Being identified as a winner is much more than an ego boost; it actually releases the four phases of winning all over again. Again, Michael Jordan is a perfect example.

Over 20 years ago, Jordan was an NBA champion, which made him idolized and imitated by many would-be NBA stars. (His patented tongue-wagging dunk can still be seen today!) But inspiring players like Kobe Bryant and LeBron James didn't stop at Phase 1. They continued to develop their own game by adding *Inspiration* and *Innovation*. Today, these NBA superstars are identified as winners, which positions them (just like Jordan in the 90's) to be imitated by young, future NBA players. And the pattern continues.

As you can see, the true beauty of The Science of Winning isn't simply winning for yourself. It's the ability to perpetuate winning to those who follow.

- Putting Science to the Test -

Now that we've discovered the four basic phases of *The Evolution of a Winner*, allow me to give you my own personal story. It's how I learned and implemented this valuable process, even at a young age.

I didn't start out as a championship fighter. Actually, I began my journey as a sixth-grade kid being picked on by others at school. To help defend myself from bullies, my mom asked if I would be interested in taking a martial arts class at our local YMCA. I jumped at the opportunity and in the summer of 1985, began walking my road.

Little did I know the hidden talent that lay dormant within me.

Within two weeks of instruction and imitating my instructor's moves, I began to rapidly outshine the 50 other kids who were chaotically, bare-knuckle fighting on the hardwood gymnasium floor. (There was nothing safe about the 80's.) After my third week, I was invited to compete in my very first tournament. Sad to say, I lost. I lost bad! It wasn't because my opponent was necessarily better, tougher, or more experienced; he simply played the game smarter than me. So I took my first loss as a lesson and returned to the gym.

Months of hard work and dedication had passed, when I was invited to participate in my second tournament. It was an opportunity for my vindication. The results? I won! As a matter of fact, I still have that trophy today, and it's just as special to me as any of my other championship medals. (The fact that it says "First Place, Pee-Wee Beginners Division" makes it even more priceless!)

Throughout my career, I didn't always win. In fact, I

lost a lot. Every time I moved up into a new age or rank bracket, there was always "the guy" who no one could beat. And, every time I employed the same strategy of winning, starting with *Imitation*. What makes this guy tick? Why does he always win? What does he do differently than everyone else? I studied how the champion won and began to imitate it. But that was only the first phase.

After imitating came *Innovation*. Where could I creatively improve until my techniques and strategies became superior? After taking many lumps and beatings—especially in new ranking categories—I came to the place where I beat "the guy," which meant now I *was* "the guy."

It was now time for Phase 3.

After a series of victories and championships, I began to transcend to the state of mind where winning was my expectation every single time I stepped into the ring. There was no doubt in my mind. It was game time, and I was going to win. Even when I didn't, it was only another opportunity to go back to the lab and start the scientific process all over again.

During my 15-year competition career, I followed this exact process over and over and over again. I became so adept at imitating and innovating, that I learned to replicate the successes of the winners two or more levels above my division. This carried me from pee-wee beginners division to regional, national, and eventually world championships in the advanced black belt divisions. In each new category, I followed the four phases of *The Evolution of a Winner: Imitation, Innovation,* and *Inspiration.*

Then came the last phase: *Identification*.

What began to eventually happen was amazing. Whenever I showed up for tournaments, certain competitors would hang their heads the minute I walked in the door. In their minds, I was already the winner. They would say things like, "Dang it! Scrivner's here. Looks like second place is the best we can do." I was already in their heads and had won the match before it even began. Why?

Winning had become my identity.

- BEING A WINNER -

Believe me, my story isn't to brag or to make myself look better than I am. As I said, I lost plenty of tournaments and suffered through more black eyes and bloody noses than you can imagine! Actually, I walked into the ring of my final world championship bout sporting two black eyes, acquired in training the week before the competition even began! I must have looked like a freak of nature, especially standing on the winner's podium with a gold medal around my neck.

The reality is, I'm a regular guy, complete with all the flaws and issues found in every other regular guy. But along the way, I've learned and implemented a system—a system of winning. I'm confident that as you begin to execute these four phases of *The Evolution of a Winner*, you'll begin your journey of winning, as well.

But, that's just the beginning!

The Science of Winning is what I call WIN*ology* 101.

The following pages contain the entire WIN*ology* process. By specifically walking out every part of this nine-step system, you'll begin to win in life at a higher level than ever before.

Before you begin, it's very important to understand that the nine steps of WIN*ology* are not in random order. They are systematic, progressive, and sequential. Each step builds upon the foundation of the previous step. *I cannot overemphasize this enough*. Resist the urge to be a know-it-all and jump ahead, skipping steps. If you do, you'll jeopardize the longevity of your winning status.

Winners are finishers, so don't quit the process. Resolve right now to finish strong. Don't quit. This system isn't only designed to teach you how to become a world-class winner, but how to remain one for the rest of your life.

So, what's the first step? It's called Urgent Excellence.

Intrigued yet? If so, keep reading. Your journey has just begun.

(Oh, and I told you that "science" wouldn't be boring, didn't I? And we're just getting started.)

3

STEP 1:
URGENT EXCELLENCE

In 2002, rap mogul, Eminem, starred in the movie, *8 Mile*.[1] The movie portrayed his beginning life struggles and the pursuit of his dreams in a profession mostly dominated by African Americans. In essence, it's a story of how a poor, fatherless, dysfunctional white kid from Detroit used The Science of Winning and the four phases of winning in *The Evolution of a Winner: Imitation, Innovation, Inspiration,* and *Identification* to move from poverty to world famous superstar status.

8 Mile not only received high critical acclaim and exploded at the box office, pulling in a record $51 million in its opening weekend, but it also launched Eminem's (born Marshall Bruce Mathers, III) music career into another stratosphere of success. Along with a top-selling movie, Eminem's hit song, "Lose Yourself," which was the theme song for the film, also gathered five Grammy Award nominations and won the 2002 Oscar for Best Original Song—the first rap song to ever receive this accolade.[2]

A part of the song says this:

"You better lose yourself in the music, the moment.

You own it, you better never let it go (go).

You only get one shot

Do not miss your chance to blow.

This opportunity comes once in a lifetime, yo

Look, if you had, one shot, or one opportunity

To seize everything you ever wanted in one moment,

Would you capture it, or just let it slip? Yo"

Not only did Eminem recognize and engage in The Science of Winning, he also unknowingly penned the anthem for the first principle of WIN*ology*: Urgent Excellence.

- GETTING TO THE ROOT -

While the term "Urgent Excellence" might be a bit foreign to you, let me give you its often used synonym: diligence. Now, I realize the word "diligence" probably ranks right up there with "science" (which is exactly why I didn't title this chapter, "Diligence!"), but let's unpack this word a bit and see how it actually is WIN*ology*'s foundational building block.

When you hear the word "diligence," you may automatically think of dotting all your "i"s and crossing all your "t"s. While it's true that diligence speaks of handling

Step 1: Urgent Excellence

your business and affairs of life with excellence, the true meaning of the word is much deeper and meaningful. Actually, one of the ancient origins of the word likens it to the concept of being sharp like a knife or tooth. However, there are other connotations that add tremendous understanding and value to its meaning.

The Latin word from which "diligence" originated is *diligentia*. It means *attentiveness or carefulness*. In the Greek language, the word translated as diligence is *spoude*, meaning *expedience, speed, or with much haste*. The French origin of the word "diligence" concurs with both the Latin and the Greek and actually merges both meanings and also adds the connotation of "speed" or "with much haste." All in all, these combined ancient meanings paint a word picture of "diligence" as: *doing things with careful attention, quickly and with no hesitation.*

This completes our linguistics lesson for this chapter!

In other words, "diligence" is Urgent Excellence—the first step of WIN*ology*.

- The Winning Combination -

If you truly desire to be a champion in certain areas of life, you must understand that being excellent in your affairs is simply not enough. Winners take the next step. They're keenly aware that excellence is connected to and fueled by a sense of urgency. This type of urgency isn't necessarily an overwhelming feeling of life and death, and certainly not anxiety or panic.

> **Urgency is an awareness of the magnitude of the moment.**

True diligence recognizes a window of opportunity at hand and does whatever it takes to seize that opportunity in the most excellent fashion.

Most people only function in half of this equation. They may be excellent, yet lack the ability to identify opportunity with a sense of urgency. On the other hand, some may recognize the opportunity at hand but fail in the excellence to actualize it. To be a winner on the level in which this book is designed, you must learn to have both elements functioning at the same time. Master artist and craftsman, Leonardo da Vinci, said it like this:

> *"I have been impressed with the urgency of doing. Knowing is not enough; we must apply. Being willing is not enough; we must do."*

Finding anyone of great accomplishments who didn't combine both the excellence of work with the urgency of recognizing a special window of opportunity is practically impossible. One of the greatest historical examples of innovation and inventive success is Thomas Edison.

Young Thomas was told by his schoolmaster that he lacked the intelligence to ever produce anything of any significance. He went on to suggest that Thomas find an occupation that could be enhanced by his outgoing personality. Edison's response to this soon-to-be-proven, grossly false assessment was simply amazing. He said:

Step 1: Urgent Excellence

"My teachers say I'm addled. My father thought I was stupid. I almost decided I must be a dunce. My mother was the making of me. She was so true, so sure of me. I felt I had someone to live for, someone I must not disappoint."

For the sake of his mother, Thomas Edison harnessed a sense of urgency and combined it with the excellence of work. The results? To this day, he still holds the record for the most patents ever issued to an individual in the U.S.: 1,093. His Urgent Excellence propelled him from "lacking intelligence" to solving problems that would change society's complete quality of life. Over the years, we have enjoyed the benefits of his many breakthrough inventions including the phonograph, practical incandescent lighting, motion pictures, and the alkaline battery, just to name a few.

Not too bad for a so-called "dunce."

Thomas Edison isn't the only one to rise from this dilemma to greatness; others have followed suit after him.

In the fifth grade, Ben was considered by his classmates and teachers to be one of the dumbest kids in his class. He even believed their opinion. One day, he

> **If you truly desire to be a champion . . . being excellent in your affairs is simply not enough.**

brought home a report card that reflected poor progress in a subject. Thinking he was, in fact, the dumbest kid in his class, Ben reasoned with his mother about his bad mark, "Mom, it doesn't matter that much." Ben's mom was of another persuasion.

Having only a third-grade education, Ben's mother knew the only way her children would escape poverty was through the means of education. She began to assist them with their assignments, insisting the boys read them to her "for their own benefit." Unbeknownst to her boys, she was actually illiterate and couldn't read the assignments herself. Her sense of Urgent Excellence outweighed her limitations.

Mama was determined that her boys would win in life.

In addition to their school assignments, she set out three rules for her two underachieving boys. Number one, they would only be allowed to watch two pre-selected TV shows per week. Number two, all homework had to be completed before any outside play or TV could commence. And number three, each boy would be required to read two library books weekly and write a report on each of them. What must have seemed like prison to her sons was an opportunity in disguise.

Honoring his mother's wishes, Ben followed the rules. It wasn't long before he began to see the fruits of his labor. One day when his teacher asked the class a question, Ben was the only student who answered correctly. Then, there was a second question. Once again, to the shock of his classmates and teacher, only one student had the correct answer—Ben.

Step 1: Urgent Excellence

Ben quickly recognized that his knowledge had come from the books he was reading. At that moment, he concluded that if he could learn a few facts from library books, what other information awaited him? For the first time in his life, Ben realized his potential of winning and with Urgent Excellence seized the opportunity.

His diligence paid off.

Not only would Ben graduate high school with high honors, he went on to receive his bachelor's degree in psychology from Yale University, followed by an M.D. from the University of Michigan Medical School.

Today, Dr. Benjamin Carson—the boy thought to be the dumbest kid in his fifth grade class—is one of the world's most renowned neurosurgeons. He has received numerous accolades, written highly acclaimed articles for leading medical journals, and has authored six best-selling books. As if these aren't enough accolades, as I pen this chapter, Dr. Carson is running for the office of the President of the United States!

These two men, along with countless others, arrived at their level of success by mastering the art of combining preparation and opportunity. They're not alone. Today—right now—you have massive opportunities in front of you, *some nearer than you think.* How do you become a winner? It starts by letting the sense of urgency be your fuel to walk through life's open doors of opportunity.

It's the beginning of WIN*ology*.

- Opportunity Knocks -

What exactly is opportunity? What does it look like? How will you know when you're facing it? While the majority of our mediocre society is simply "waiting for their ship to come in," world-class winners view opportunity differently.

Thomas Edison said it best:

> *"Opportunity is missed by most people, because it is dressed in overalls and looks like work."*

To win in life, you must first open your eyes, recognize what's before you, and then get to work. It's having a sense of Urgent Excellence.

In the spring of 1993, I was faced with such a window.

The Taekwondo Federation, with which I was associated, was in the process of building a team to represent the U.S. at the Global Taekwondo Federation World Championships. The competition was to be held later that year in Moscow, Russia. The good news was that the 153-pound weight class was wide open. The bad news was, I weighed 178 pounds at the time. With barely three months to lose 25 pounds, I was faced with a decision.

Dropping that much weight, in that amount of time, while still maintaining a world-class edge and skill set for the tryouts, seemed practically impossible. My decision came down to some fundamental questions I had to answer. Would I make excuses of how that was too much

Step 1: Urgent Excellence

weight to lose on such short notice? Would I stay comfortable and content with my national titles or respond to the dream of a world championship? Would I leave my comfort zone and rise to the challenge, applying myself to the most rigorous training regimen I had ever experienced? The decision was mine.

I chose the path of diligence.

> **To win in life, you must first open your eyes, recognize what's before you, and then get to work.**

The sense of urgency compounded and fueled my desire for excellence. Something within me confirmed that this was a golden opportunity that could alter my life forever. In the words of Eminem, I truly had "one shot, one opportunity to seize everything I ever wanted." This was my open door.

So, I buckled down and went to work.

- Life on a Mission -

Knowing the task in front of me, I immediately jumped into a rigorous, six-day-a-week, insane training routine. Intensive fight training, technical drill work, weight lifting, and hours upon hours of cardio were my daily regimen. My diet also underwent a major change. No sugar, no bad fats, no sodas, no deserts—which also meant no fun! Quickly, the baby fat started melting off my

19 year-old frame to the point where people were concerned for my health. Many tried to talk me out of my decision, claiming the intense schedule and rapid weight loss were too extreme and unsafe. But, I was obsessed with my goal and unwilling to even entertain distractions. My decision had been made.

I was on a mission.

By the summer of 1993, I looked like a rail! My entire wardrobe hung off my body like a kid wearing his daddy's clothes. However, I felt better than ever.

As if the challenge to train and win a spot on the U.S. national team wasn't grueling enough, the actual tryouts came right on the heels of a six-day, intensive black belt training camp . . . held outdoors in the Arkansas summer heat. The final morning of that camp, I was tested for my third degree black belt. The testing lasted more than four solid hours and was held outdoors under the intense Ozark sun. Timing wasn't on my side, *but diligence was.*

Tryout day finally came and I showed up with two black eyes and bruises all over my body—battle scars from the previous six days of training and testing. I will never forget that Sunday afternoon in Little Rock, AR. Little did I know I would be the youngest competitor to try out, not to mention one of the least experienced. But, I had made my decision. Win, lose, or draw, this was my time to lay everything on the line.

At the end of the day, with a severely beat up body and two black eyes, I scored more overall points than 38 of the 40 competitors. This locked me in for the number

Step 1: Urgent Excellence

two spot on the team. Diligence had won. My life would never be the same.

That year in Russia, I won two silver medals at the world championships. Along with the medals, our team had the honor of being the first American athletes to ever compete in the Olympic stadium. The stadium was built for the 1980 Moscow Olympics, but the U.S. boycotted their participation. Our team also witnessed a very significant occurrence—both for the country of Russia and, symbolically, for my personal life.

The Russian Parliament had initiated a coup against President Boris Yeltsin, who was attempting to dissolve the Soviet's power and introduce democracy to Russia. In the early morning of October 4, 1993, the Russian army, in response to President Yeltsin's impeachment, stormed the Parliament and restored Yeltsin to power. In their pursuit, Russian tanks drove directly in front of our hotel—a sight our team will remember forever.

Little did we know that history was unfolding right in front of our eyes. Some historians have called it the deadliest day in Moscow since the Revolution of 1917. Freedom was coming to Russia. But that wasn't all. Due to my own newfound diligence, freedom was coming to me, as well.

- Seize the Moment -

This is part of my journey of winning, but what about you? How many times have you sensed a window of opportunity and watched it pass you by? I know I've

> **Writing down your goals makes them official and is the first step of diligence.**

missed a couple of boats along the way. There's nothing we can do about opportunities missed, but there certainly is something you can do about the next one: Seize it with Urgent Excellence!

Famous English author and speaker, Leonard Ravenhill, once said one of the most profound statements concerning the subject of opportunity and Urgent Excellence:

"The opportunity of a lifetime must be seized within the lifetime of the opportunity."

Read this quote a few times, slowly. Let its powerful truth sink into your mind and spirit. Every opportunity has a timeframe. For me, that one golden opportunity had a shelf life of three months. After that time, the window would close. Walking through this particular part of my journey, I learned three valuable lessons of Urgent Excellence:

- It *recognizes* an opportunity.
- It *responds* swiftly to conquer the moment.
- It produces great *rewards*.

Step 1: Urgent Excellence

Are there any areas in your life—maybe an area you feel a touch of destiny or natural giftedness—where you sense a window of opportunity opening? Is there a feeling of urgency to not let this one slip away? Now, will you capture the moment or let it slip away? WIN*ologists* do the former, and build a life beyond their wildest dreams.

You have no control over when the next window of opportunity will open. However, what you can control is your personal diligence to be ready when it does. You must harness the sense of urgency and let it drive you towards excellence.

- Get Started -

Urgent Excellence isn't difficult to begin. As a matter of fact, you can start right now. It's simple. Notice I didn't say it was easy, just simple. Let's get started.

What dreams do you have for your life right now? What is your heart's greatest desire? Do you have educational, relational, financial, or vocational goals? Then stop right now, take a sheet of paper, your iPad, or your WIN*ology* journal, and list them out one-by-one. Can you do that? If you can, congratulations. Just doing this single exercise places you in the top five percent of people in the world who want to accomplish a goal. Ninety-five percent never accomplish this first step.

Here's a little secret: Until you write down your desires and goals and post them in a place where they are in front of your eyes every day, they will migrate to some dark corner in the back of your mind.

Every step of WIN*ology* will carry specific assignments. Commit to allowing the next eight WIN*ology* steps to transform your positive disciplines into other areas of your life. Deciding to win is the first step to winning.

STEP 1
- URGENT EXCELLENCE -
ASSIGNMENTS

- Take a complete inventory of your life right now. First, write down the areas where you're the *most* diligent and feel like you best practice Urgent Excellence. (Maybe it's in the area of personal health, personal finances, or the development of family and personal relationships.)

- Take a moment and celebrate the areas where you're exercising diligence and are seeing positive results.

- Now, write down the areas where you need to be more urgent and excellent. Be really honest. Take a good look at your answers.

Step 1: Urgent Excellence

> ♦ Write a personal statement of affirmation for your victories followed by a statement regarding your decisions to improve.

Now that you have a grasp of Urgent Excellence, it's time for the next crucial step in WIN*ology*: Positive Conviction. In the following chapter, you're going to see how to design your future from the inside out—how to "think and believe" like the world-class winner you were born to be.

Opportunity is knocking? Are you ready? Do you feel a sense of urgency?

Then, let's go!

WIN*OLOGY* 101

STEP 1
URGENT EXCELLENCE

4

STEP 2:
POSITIVE CONVICTION

O ne of my all-time favorite quotes comes from legendary artist, Pablo Picasso. He said:

"My mother stated to me, 'If you are a soldier, you will become a general. If you are a monk, you will become the Pope.' Instead, I was a painter and became Picasso."

Much like Thomas Edison and Dr. Benjamin Carson, Picasso had a mother who believed in him and instilled within him a deep sense of faith—a faith that he could do and become something great. This positive belief system shaped Picasso's life from early childhood and powered him onward to success. What is the belief system?

WIN*ology* Step 2: Positive Conviction.

The word, "conviction," usually doesn't carry many optimistic connotations. For example, when someone is convicted of a crime, punishment for their actions follows suit. We've all heard the old adage, "Do the crime, pay the time." In that light, conviction is not a good thing.

In the same manner, if someone participates in an unethical or immoral activity, they can be convicted in their heart or conscience of their wrongdoing. For years I've heard people say, "I knew it was wrong the second I did it." They were convicted of their actions. However, conviction doesn't always have to be viewed in a negative light. You *can* experience Positive Conviction.

> **What you believe, you become.**

For the context of this step, let's look at another meaning of the word, "conviction." It's *a firmly held belief or opinion; the quality of showing that one is firmly convinced of what one believes or says.* Positive Conviction, or the power of your own belief system, is the place where greatness is conceived. Before you become a champion in your desired area, you first must see yourself as such and firmly believe you are destined to win. It's true: What you believe, you become.

This chapter is primarily designed to accomplish two things:

1. Examine the power of your own personal belief system and...

2. Harness the power of positivity and release it into your life.

Step 2: Positive Conviction

So, if you're ready, let's jump into WIN*ology* Step 2.

- The Seedbed -

One of Henry Ford's most classic quotes is: "Whether you think you can or think you can't—you are right." The truth is, Henry was right! What Mr. Ford really did was to rephrase an ancient proverb, written thousands of years before his time. The proverb so precisely says:

"As a man thinks in his heart, so is he . . ."[1]

This proverb opens up an interesting dialogue. One might quip, "That's ridiculous. We don't think with our heart, we think with our minds." However, the ancients may have had more insight than initially understood.

Dr. Caroline Leaf, an expert in neurology and behavioral science, reported some fascinating findings in her book, *Who Switched Off My Brain*.[2] She documents how modern scientists have now discovered that the human heart contains over 40,000 neurons, and it can actually initiate conversations with the brain. This discovery is incredibly intriguing, for it gives a whole new meaning to statements like, "Follow your heart," or, "Guard your heart."

According to medical science research, it seems that the heart is much more than a pump to push blood throughout our bodies. It may be, in fact, the seedbed of our most powerful desires and truest sense of our identity.

Many years ago my friend, Nick, had a heart transplant. You can only imagine the shock and scare associated with such a traumatic surgery, especially given Nick was only in his late 20's. Before and after his procedures, I spent a great deal of time with Nick in which we shared many interesting conversations.

One of the most unique occurrences comes to mind.

After his surgery was complete, Nick and I were having one of our usual talks, when all of a sudden, it turned into a moment of confession. Nick was very confused concerning some of his post-surgery thoughts and feelings. Specifically, he was experiencing very powerful and graphic dreams unlike anything he'd ever encountered. He described them more as memories than dreams, mainly because these instances were too specific and detailed to only come from his subconscious imagination. In addition, Nick was also having intense cravings for Mexican food—a taste that had never registered on his palette in times past.

But, these weren't the strangest of reactions.

Along with his graphic dreams and newfound love of fajitas, Nick was also dealing with a much more serious issue. It seemed he was having random thoughts and attractions to Hispanic women—again, way out of his norm as Nick was a very committed, African-American family man with a beautiful wife and children.

Step 2: Positive Conviction

These very peculiar thoughts and feelings were so troublesome that Nick began to probe the surgeons for answers. Why was he having intense dreams? Why the love for Mexican food? Where in the world were the thoughts and attractions for Hispanic women coming from? (Thank God, his sweet wife, Cynthia, was of Panamanian decent or Nick may have needed much more than a new heart!) The surgeon's answers, though bringing clarity, were nothing less than baffling.

The heart Nick was given came from a 40 year-old Hispanic man!

Not only was he the recipient of a muscle to transport life-giving blood to his body, Nick also received many of his donor's memories, tastes, and interests. It seems the ancient proverb, "As a man thinks in his heart,"[3] is more accurate than previously understood. Our human heart has the power to navigate the outcome of our lives more than we ever realized.

It is the seedbed of our strongest beliefs.

- It's Time to Choose -

Even though I've never had a heart transplant, I am living proof that true convictions can only be birthed from your bedrock beliefs—your belief in yourself, your life, and your potential. Thankfully, I was blessed with two of the greatest "believe in yourself" mentors one could ever dream of: my parents.

Throughout my life, and in every area of life, my

parents infused me with a sense of positivity and personal belief that launched me into arenas of success I may have never obtained on my own. There was never a time when they didn't reinforce that belief system. I'm so thankful for their influence, and I try to never take it for granted.

My memories are flooded with statements like, "We believe in you, Joel. We know you can do it," and, "Joel, you can accomplish anything you set your mind to. You just have to decide and then act on it." My mother, apparently convinced I was touched with a sense of divine destiny, even called me "The Golden Boy," for crying out loud! Talk about setting a kid up for megalomania. And to top it all off, my grandma (while so awkwardly pinching my cheeks and shaking my face) called me "pretty boy" every time she saw me.

This was my life, but what about yours? Maybe you experienced a similar upbringing. Then again, yours could have been vastly opposite. No matter where you've come from, or what influence, if any, your parents held in your life, today you are faced with a decision. You can allow a constant string of excuses for not winning—primarily based on what you did or didn't receive as a child—to come out of your mouth. Or, you can make the decision to acquire and develop a belief system that wasn't offered to you in childhood. Whatever the case, *now* is the time to choose. The world-class winning version of you hangs in the balance.

STEP 2: POSITIVE CONVICTION

- BECOMING A POSITIVE GENIUS -

It's no secret that we live in an increasingly negative world. Just watch the evening news. You'll quickly learn that good news doesn't sell. With headlines dominated by scandals and tragedies, one almost needs a bottle of Xanax just to make it through the 10 o'clock news! In the light of this reality, this WIN*ology* fact remains paramount:

You can never overemphasize the power of positivity with regard to your personal beliefs.

An essential component in Positive Conviction is that each of us must learn how to harness and maximize the power of the positive truths in our lives. Plainly spoken, amid the cesspool of negativity, we must become positive geniuses. That's right, a positive genius. We must make an asserted effort, each and every day, to build a place of powerful positivity. Does that sound too difficult? Think again.

According to scientific studies, positivity is a learned skill. It's been proven to be one of the premier ingredients that reside in the world's most successful and satisfied people. My eyes were recently enlightened to this concept through an author I've grown to admire, Shawn Achor.

Achor is an expert in the new and quickly emerging field of positive psychology. His writings, which confirm this WIN*ology* principle, offer incredible scientific validation to what I've believed and proven all along to be true. I would highly recommend adding his works to your WINology library.

So, how do you become a positive genius? Achor discloses a powerful key.

For decades, optimists have often been ridiculed and belittled by both realists and pessimists for their "so-called" lack of logic. However, modern breakthroughs in psychology, neurology, and behavioral science are proving the power of positivity to be not only real, but a requirement for success. As Achor reveals, finding a true positive reality, even in the midst of the most horrible of circumstances, is the key to moving beyond tragedy and finding yourself back in a healthy place in life.

For centuries, society has told us, "If you become successful, then you'll be happy." The problem with this theory is simple and tragic: Our modern culture's definition of "happiness" is a constantly moving target. Consequently, millions of people, who haven't been able to capture this evasive euphoria, have been left with overwhelming feelings of hopelessness, specifically of ever achieving success or happiness. But the tide is turning.

Achor brilliantly equates this shift in modern psychology to Nicholas Copernicus' world-changing discovery in 1543 that the earth revolves around the sun, instead of the sun revolving around the earth. The same is true with happiness/success:

Success revolves around happiness; happiness doesn't revolve around success.

Step 2: Positive Conviction

When you learn to be happy, regardless of opposition or circumstance, success tends to follow as the natural by-product.

So, what do positive geniuses do? It's simple. They position themselves to win by learning to be happy, and by finding true, positive realities in any situation or circumstance...

Even in the midst of the most horrific occurrences.

- The Day the Sky Fell -

With all my martial arts championships, along with a collection of winning in many other areas of life under my belt, nothing could have prepared my wife, Jennifer, and me for November 16, 2002.

It's the day the sky fell.

On that day, we lost our precious 18 month-old daughter, O'Neal. She was our first baby, our greatest prize. In an instant, our world seemed to fall apart and disintegrate all around us. We were living every parent's nightmare of epic proportions. For the first time in my life, I had fought a battle I couldn't win. There was no rematch ... no sequel ... no next time. O'Neal was gone, and our seemingly perfect world crumbled before our very eyes.

Now, hopefully you have a better understanding of my statement, "I haven't always won." But no loss ever hurt to the depths of this one. At times, it was practically unbearable.

For eight months, O'Neal battled. She was such a fighter. Her name even meant, "The Champion." Day after day, we watched our baby girl helplessly suffer. Then, she died. It was the darkest day of our young married life. Our hopes and dreams of a miracle were shattered right in front of our eyes. How could anything positive possibly come from this tragedy?

Unbelievably, it did.

By determining to find happiness, no matter the situation, I found the Positive Conviction principle to be true. In the midst of our most horrific time, when our faith was devastated, so many good things occurred. Sure, it was difficult to recognize them amongst all the rubble and chaos, but they were there. We just had to find them.

For starters, Jennifer and I quickly came to realize the host of genuine friends and loved ones that were in our lives. In a time where we felt the most isolated and alone, in reality we were surrounded by incredible people. These God-sends battled for, and with, us on a daily basis. This, within itself, was enough positivity to get us through. But there was more.

During this time, I also came to know a faith that was bigger than the stark reality which daily stared me in the face. This faith in God would serve as the premier anchor in my life and the life of my family.

Yet, another positive occurred with Jennifer and me. We were told that 90% of couples who suffer the loss of a child, divorce within three to five years. We were no better than anyone else who had previously walked

Step 2: Positive Conviction

through this nightmare. But when we heard this statistic, it released a life-altering, positive decision within us: We would be part of the 10% who make it! In the end, we came to understand that we could not only endure the most devastating experience life could throw our way, but we could make it through to the other side, as well.

Our decision to stay together, no matter what, wasn't always easy to sustain. In fact, at times, it was brutal. (We will talk more about this in the next chapter.) One of the major challenges we quickly encountered was the fact that we both grieved differently. This fact, coupled with the negative truth that two people living in survival mode are both extremely selfish, made our road even more difficult. Nevertheless, we didn't give up.

Jennifer and I survived not only our daughter's death from cancer, but the cancer of any marriage: selfishness. In our midnight hours, we held on to three things: our faith, our decision, and each other. Our new, true, positive reality was that, despite our pain and confusion, we deeply loved each other and knew our Positive Conviction would see us through. It did! We recently celebrated our 20th wedding anniversary.

Here's to 20 more!

- Positive/Negative -

The power of Positive Conviction is the initial ingredient to winning. Learning how to harness and release the power of finding true, positive realities, even in the

> The power of Positive Conviction is the initial ingredient to winning.

midst of struggles, will position you to win. How do you accomplish this feat? It all starts between your ears—with the way you think.

We've all been taught that thoughts are nothing more than immaterial wisps. Nothing could be further from the truth. Thoughts are biochemical and electromagnetic entities. Our thoughts and beliefs, though not physically visible or tangible, are actually evidential and substantial in nature. They are very real. They are also very, very powerful.

Dr. Caroline Leaf, whom I mentioned earlier, offers some amazing insights on this subject.

According to Dr. Leaf, scientific discovery is actually proving that one can "think" themselves well or sick, depending on one's emotional and intellectual health. Positive or negative thoughts release one of two things into our bodies: life-giving hormones (a.k.a. healing chemicals) or toxic poisons that can literally result in physical sickness. According to new scientific discoveries, the cycles of negative thoughts activate a series of self-poisoning, which can cause perpetual physical sickness as well as increased negativity (the cancer of the soul). But there's another option.

By capturing a negative thought or imagination in the

STEP 2: POSITIVE CONVICTION

moment of conception and reprogramming it with a new positive reality, you can stop the cycle of poison. In essence, you have the power to thwart negative thoughts, which yield sickness and stress, and replace them with positive thoughts that produce physical healing cycles. Leaf also notes how scientists have subsequently discovered that this process can systematically increase our intelligence by up to 70%! Talk about positive genius. This is the power of Positive Conviction at work.

But the choice is yours.

Now, let's break this all down. At any given moment and in every circumstance, both positive and negative realities simultaneously exist. They're both equally true and powerful. Here's the good news: You have a choice! Whichever one you choose to embrace—the positive or the negative—will determine your outcome and future success.

Jennifer and I could have so easily blamed God, blamed each other, or blamed medical science for the death of our baby. Believe me, the temptation to give into negative thoughts bombarded our minds every day. But we had made a decision, based on our true, positive reality. Even in the midst of death, positive thoughts were there—we just had to *choose* to find them and then activate them in our lives. Was it easy? Never. Are we glad we did it? Absolutely, and we're eternally grateful. Today, we are living our dream with our two beautiful girls, Sydney and Blakely.

It's true, you do have the power to choose a new, true,

positive reality and begin to reshape your life from the inside out. The proverb was right and has been scientifically-proven through years of research: As you think, so are you.[4] My family is a living testimony that Positive Conviction isn't some astrophysics mumbo jumbo.

It works!

- Put it in Action -

Over many years of living through triumph and tragedy, I've found two very powerful tools that have helped to keep me in a constant state of positivity—journaling and gratefulness. Let's look at both of these.

Journaling. Practically no other discipline is as incredible for your soul and empowering for your creativity as journaling. It's been one of the most healing and freeing activities I've developed in the last 20 years. Journaling is the outlet that has carried me through the worst of times and launched me into the best of times. It also kept me in a constant flow of positivity.

I initially started to journal some of my thoughts, prayers, and experiences, simply to leave a legacy for my future generations. I had no idea how much it would eventually shape my own life. Untold amounts of *Inspiration* have come to me through my own private dialogues. As a matter of fact, this book was birthed from many of my journal entries.

Step 2: Positive Conviction

Every great scientist keeps a log of their research and findings, using them as a reference from time to time. WIN*ologists* should do the exact same thing by journaling daily. Finding a positive outlet for your emotions and thoughts is invaluable in your quest to become the world-class winning version of yourself. Not to mention, it's one of the best ways to document your progress over time.

> Whichever one you choose to embrace—the positive or the negative—will determine your outcome and future success.

Many of the greatest minds of our time, from scientists and inventors to our founding fathers and scholars, have been rabid journalers. Make it a part of your regular routine.

Gratefulness. Gratefulness is one of the greatest powers for sustainable positivity. Living in a constant state of gratitude not only changes your outlook on life, but also keeps you surrounded with Positive Conviction. On the other hand, ungratefulness leads to bitterness, which is a poison to your system. My grandmother used to say, "Bitterness rots the bones." She was right.

Complaining about your life will never produce positivity. I once saw an older man in a restaurant and, out of courtesy, greeted him by asking, "How are you, sir?" His answer will stick with me forever. "Can't complain, son. And even if I did, what good would it do?" Yet another great nugget of wisdom.

As a WIN*ologist*, make a daily habit to stop and reflect on who and what you're grateful for. Then, write those down in your journal. Next, take it a step further by sending a quick text message or e-mail or make a phone call to someone, telling them why you're thankful for them. You'll be amazed at the level of happiness and positivity this brings into your life and the life of others as you pay forward Positive Conviction.

- You're on Your Way! -

Let's recap and finish out this chapter.

First, you must learn to find the *true*, positive reality in every situation. False hyper-positivity with no basis in truth can actually produce more harm than good. Recognize the negative, but don't camp there. Choose to find the true positives that also exist. This incredible skill comes more naturally to some, but can be learned and perfected by all.

Second, make a decision to embrace that new, true, positive reality relentlessly and ride it all the way out of your negative situation. Along with many other things, it will help you formulate a plan of action to move forward, which is the next WIN*ology* step.

On the next page, you'll find your Step 2: Positive Conviction Assignments.

STEP 2
- POSITIVE CONVICTION -
ASSIGNMENTS

- Take a moment and look at your current situation. Take as much time as you need.
- Locate and write down *every* positive thing, experience, and individual in your life right now. Those are your lifelines.
- Starting today, write down at least one thing/person for which or whom you're grateful.
- Take 30 seconds and send the person a message, expressing your gratitude.
- List every negative situation happening in your life. Now, search through each one and find the true, positive realities. They are there. You just have to find them. Write those positive realities next to the negative situation and *focus on the true positives*.

Congratulations, you're evolving into the champion you were created to be! More importantly, winning is becoming your state of mind and truly your new identity. I'd say that WIN*ology* suits you well! Now, on to the good stuff.

Your journey is only beginning.

WIN*OLOGY* 101

STEP 1
URGENT EXCELLENCE

STEP 2
POSITIVE CONVICTION

5

STEP 3:
DECISIVE ACTION

Many things about my childhood greatly affected my life forever—some good, others served as great learning opportunities. One of the most impacting wasn't a talk, a lecture, or a congratulations from my parents or coaches; it was an old wooden sign my dad handmade and hung right above our kitchen door.

Every day as I ran out to catch the school bus or hang out with friends, I would read these words:

"Do what you can, where you are, with what you have."

I would later learn these words didn't originate with my dad, but were penned by the great President Theodore Roosevelt. No matter who wrote them, one thing was for sure: They'd have a greater impact on my life than I could've ever imagined. With that phrase, all excuses were erased. There was always something I *could* do. Now, it was up to me—I simply had to do it.

I had to activate WIN*ology* Step 3: Decisive Action.

- Man Up -

Before you move into this step, let me first give you a disclaimer: This is where the rubber meets the road! As my dad used to say, "Joel, it's time to either put up or shut up." Such is the case with Decisive Action. It will require some intestinal fortitude—a.k.a. guts!

Studying the key components found in the attributes of true winners, I discovered a quality all great champions possess—virtue. Actually, "virtue" derives from the Greek word, *arête*. When you think about it, the Greek Imperial era contains more stories of virtue, valor, and heroism than any other time in history.

One of the most famous of all ancient Greek writers, Homer, used the word, *arête,* quite frequently in many different instances and with various connotations. Interestingly, Homer's use of the word wasn't gender specific. Not only did he describe Spartan warriors and Trojan heroes as virtuous, some of his major female characters, like Penelope, the wife of Odysseus, were also *arête*—exceedingly honorable and brave.

A bit more digging into the roots of this word revealed the simplicity, yet power, of this WIN*ology* step.

Arête is composed of an evolving string of two words.

Step 3: Decisive Action

The first word, "arren," is the word for *man*, more specifically, the characteristics of manliness or valiance in battle. The second word is "airo," which means *up or elevated*. Put these two root words together, and you get "man up!" Seeing this caused a light bulb to go off in my head.

Anyone who desires to be a champion in life must possess *arête*: virtue and exemplary bravery. As related to WIN*ology* Step 3, Decisive Action isn't always easy. Talk is cheap. Anyone can "talk the talk," but are you willing to "walk the walk?" Are you ready to exude the qualities of epic heroes, taking the necessary steps of action to turn your dreams into reality? Are you ready to add *arête* as part of your intrinsic nature? If so, then it's time to "man up," or "woman up," if you will, and start putting actions to what you already believe.

It's time for Decisive Action.

- Mind Your Mouth -

As a WIN*ologist*, one of the most effective decisions you'll ever make is controlling the words that come out of your mouth. Maintaining the power of positivity is a lifelong process. As long as there are negative thoughts (which is forever), you'll be perpetually and systematically capturing those thoughts and reprogramming them into new, true, positive ones. Positive thinking is the foundation for winning, but the next step is equally as important:

Taking Decisive Action to speak positively.

The words which proceed out of your mouth, will either construct or destroy your Positive Conviction infrastructure. What you speak about yourself and your future will come to pass. Why? Mainly, it's because your voice is the most powerful voice to your psyche. Think about it. You've been listening to your own voice all your life, which has trained your conscious and sub-conscious mind to trust it explicitly. Your next step to winning will be determined by one of two issues:

- Will you adhere to and speak according to your new, true, positive realities?
- Will you continue in your old patterns of thought and speech?

The words you speak will either construct or destroy your Positive Conviction infrastructure.

Dr. Caroline Leaf, whom you met in the previous chapter, has revealed overwhelming scientific data on this subject. According to her findings, the words which come out of our mouth actually frame our world. With this thought in mind, how much should we value the power of our own words? They carry the potential to build or destroy our relationships, our self-worth, and even our future.

Step 3: Decisive Action

One of the best proving grounds for the power of words is within a marriage relationship. Anyone who's married or has ever been in a committed relationship knows how damaging saying the wrong thing at the wrong time can be. We've all mis-spoken and ruined a good moment—or worse, wound up in the doghouse!

Speaking negatively comes so naturally—to the point that we can easily justify our destructive comments.

Have you ever caught yourself speaking negatively to someone (maybe yourself) and then justified it by saying, "I'm just keeping it real," or "I'm just being brutally honest"? Of course. We all have. I'm as guilty as anyone of popping off and saying something that produced the exact opposite results I desired. But to live as a world-class winner, these justifications must cease. You must "mind your mouth" and create new, true, positive *declarations,* which seamlessly match your Positive Convictions.

> **A positive mindset will never produce a winning lifestyle if it never extends past your mouth.**

Hear and never forget this WIN*ology* truth: A positive mindset will never produce a winning lifestyle if it never extends past your mouth.

Positive Conviction is maintained, validated, and released into action by positive declarations. Do you want to win in life in first-rate form? Then it's simple. First, think true and positive thoughts. Second, make a critical, decisive action to mind your mouth and declare your new, true, positive future.

- Something has to Change -

I will never forget the day the lesson of making positive declarations hit home with me. Regretfully, it wasn't in one of my finest moments, but the message will remain in my mind forever.

After the death of our daughter, my relationship with Jennifer was severely strained. Yes, we had found our new, true positives and had taken Decisive Action to stay married no matter what. Still, those decisions didn't stop the struggles from taking their toll on us.

Not long after O'Neal died, we both severely struggled to find our identities and to figure out what we believed about ourselves, our future, and even God. During this time, our interactions were often volatile. So many hurtful and poisonous things spewed out of our mouths. We were both torn up on the inside and, at the same time, were tearing each other apart on the outside.

For us to make it, something had to change.

One night, right in the middle of some very heated exchanges, I decided to say something totally different than my usual angry return verbal volley. In the middle of our conversation, my rebuttal was instead kind, positive declarations over my beautiful, yet at the time angry,

Step 3: Decisive Action

hurting wife. Instead of reacting out of my own anger and emotions, I countered with affirming statements which aligned with Jennifer's true character—the beautiful, kind, affectionate, understanding, patient, doting, love of my life, Jennifer.

Still furious—and now shocked beyond belief—she cocked her head like a puppy who'd just heard a strange noise. With a wild look in her eyes, she responded, "Joel, are you speaking some of that positive confession crap over me right now?" "Yeah, baby," I replied. "The other stuff wasn't working so I figured I'd try something new."

In an instant, all the tension broke.

Immediately, we both started laughing and then apologized for our hurtful statements. For the first time in a very long time, that moment actually felt as though we had come back into our right minds. What started out to be a verbal assault-fest turned into a great night, with a lesson I'll never forget:

There's power in the Decisive Action of minding your mouth.

- Sweet as Sugar -

Walker Smith Jr. was born in Detroit, MI, May 3, 1921. At 12 years old, Walker's parents separated and he moved with his mother to the New York City neighborhood of Harlem. Smith's original desire was to be a doctor, but after dropping out of high school in the ninth grade, his passion changed...

To boxing.

At 15 years of age, Walker attempted to enter his first boxing tournament. Much to his dismay, he wasn't allowed in the tournament because he didn't own an AAU membership card—one of the requirements to participate. To make things even worse, the minimum age for AAU membership was 18 years old—three years older than Smith's current age. Not to be denied his dream, Walker Smith found a way. He took Decisive Action!

Walker found a way to become an AAU member by borrowing a birth certificate from his of-age friend, Ray Robinson. Throughout his time in AAU, people never knew his real name, just his alias. It didn't take long for "Ray Robinson" to turn heads as his boxing skills were superlative to all the others.

Beyond the moxie to "borrow" a friend's identity, Robinson took further action to reach his goal: He hit the gym. Before jumping into any tournaments, he spent several months training for hours a day, jumping rope, shadowboxing, hitting mitts, and sparring. Some months later, at a fight held in Watertown, NY, a lady in the audience told Robinson that he was "sweet as sugar." Thus, Walker Smith, Jr. became known as "Sugar" Ray Robinson.

The rest is history.

With a professional record of 128 wins, one loss, and two draws, Sugar Ray Robinson is arguably the greatest pound-for-pound fighter in boxing history. Compared to current legend, Floyd Mayweather's impressive 48-0 record, Sugar Ray Robinson won 91 consecutive fights—84 of

Step 3: Decisive Action

the victories by way of knockout—without a loss! There's no doubt, Mayweather is great, but there's simply no comparison.

Sugar Ray is the hero of every great boxer in modern history. How did he become such a decorated champion? The WIN*ology* way: by seeing a window of opportunity; believing true, positive realities about himself and his talents; and then taking Decisive Action. Robinson was convinced of the power of positive declarations, as seen in one of his most famous quotes:

> *"To be a champ you have to believe in yourself when nobody else will."*

Sugar Ray is right. Fans are fickle. Co-workers can be selfish and bosses unappreciative. Sometimes, you have to cheer yourself on! It's the power of positive confession. To be world-class in your pursuit, positive declarations, as vital as they are to winning, aren't enough on their own. Decisive Actions must accompany.

Robinson believed and spoke positively, but took other calculated steps of Decisive Action on his road to greatness. One of those actions was the decision to relentlessly train for decades, regardless of the obstacles, injuries, and setbacks. It's a common ingredient among the "best of the best"—the willingness to do what others will not do. The "best" make a decision to work harder, smarter, and longer which separates them from the "rest."

> The "greats" ... decide to do what others won't, so they can obtain the status others don't.

A long-time friend of mine, Dominique, played professional basketball for many years. During his time in the pros, he interacted with many coaches and players who had firsthand knowledge of one of the game's greatest—Kobe Bryant.

Contrary to popular belief, Kobe doesn't spend his off-season lounging by the pool, cruising around all day in exotic sports cars, and throwing his money away on frivolous entertainment. If you want to find this multi-world-champion during those five months, you'll have to look in the gym! That's where you'll find him, six days a week, six hours a day—running, jumping, lifting, dribbling, shooting, scrimmaging, and studying his opponents. When you think about it, there's not much "off" in Kobe's off-season.

While others are hitting the snooze button, winners take Decisive Action to work . . . and work . . . and work! The "greats" aren't great just because of talent; they decide to do what others won't, so they can obtain the status others don't.

Step 3: Decisive Action

- Time to Act -

As I said previously, walking out WIN*ology* Step 3—living a life of virtue reflected by Decisive Action—will not come easy. It requires bold steps to accomplish. This is the place where it's time to put your money where your mouth is—time to move beyond being just a dreamer and do whatever it takes to start living your dreams right now.

There's nothing wrong with dreaming, as long as you wake up from your dreams and put action to them! Without practical application and Decisive Action regarding your positive belief system, your dreams will only remain fantasies and fairy tales. Beliefs and Positive Convictions are desperately needed; however, no matter how positive they may be, without action they are dead and worthless.

Self-help guru and multi-New York Times best-selling author, Tony Robbins, said it best:

"Remember, a real decision is measured by the fact that you've taken new action. If there's no action, you haven't truly decided."

What time is it? It's time to act!

One of the greatest joys of my life is to coach people into greatness. So, allow me to jump into the coaching mode for just a moment and bring these principles to where you live.

For you to accomplish your dreams or goals, you must lay out your precise action steps. Do you need to learn or develop a new skill? Is going back to school or obtaining another certification the next step? Do you need to meet with someone to help design a blueprint for your dream, so you can start moving forward? For you to hit your fitness goal, do you need to join a gym? Hire a trainer? Buy a bike? Throw out all the Ding Dongs, Twinkies, and soft drinks from the pantry? (This might be the boldest step of all!)

Whatever the case may be, the beginning point of your success is to stop talking and start doing.

Go back to your WIN*ology* journal and start making a list. Do it right now! Write out what Decisive Actions you need to take in each area of your life. What can you do today, tomorrow, or the next day? What can you accomplish by next week? Where do you need to be by the end of the month? Let's go! If you want world-class winning in certain areas, then let's do it, together.

- THE TIME IS NOW -

Okay, step back and breathe for a moment. We've already covered a lot of information, and we still have six more WIN*ology* steps to go. If you're feeling overloaded and not quite ready to start taking bold action steps, that's perfectly fine. Spend some more time in these first three steps to build your confidence, establish your new, true, positives, and prepare your Decisive Action

Step 3: Decisive Action

plan. Moving forward before you're truly ready will only produce frustration; however, many times, final preparation only comes as you take action and move forward in your quest.

On the other hand...

If you know your dreams and you're ready to take Decisive Action, my question is simple: What are you waiting for? Remember, WIN*ology* Step 1 is Urgent Excellence—recognizing and capturing moments of opportunity. You have great gifts inside of you that can and will make the world and people around you better. There's no time to waste; this is your time to act. Abraham Lincoln said it like this:

> **"Things may come to those who wait, but only the things left by those who hustle."**

Maybe you're afraid of failure. Welcome to the club! The truth is, everyone is afraid to fail at one point or another. But remember, even if you fail, it's merely a learning opportunity for you—a true winner—to regroup and rally back to victory. Let's make a Decisive Action declaration, right now: "I'm not afraid of failure. Even when I fail, I win, because I learn from my failures. I'm a winner. Winning is what I do."

It may sound corny, but say it anyway. Say it every day, multiple times a day if need be. You're framing your world for success.

Now, on to your WIN*ology* Step 3 Assignments:

STEP 3
- Decisive Action -
Assignments

- Take a moment and write in your WIN*ology* journal every area in which you desire to win big. Be specific. (Your marriage, relationship with your kids, vocation, or relationship with co-workers, hobbies, personal fitness, start-up or home-based business, etc.) Be specific about what you want to see accomplished in these areas.

- Create positive declarations for every area you have listed. This is your initial Decisive Action, to "create your world with your words." It absolutely works and will change your life from the inside out.

- Take some of the declarations—the ones that are top priorities—and post them in strategic places where you will see them throughout the day. Your refrigerator, bathroom mirror, dashboard of your car, and computer wallpaper are some great options. (I have a sign on my bathroom mirror with the five most important things I do every day.)

Step 3: Decisive Action

> - What other steps of Decisive Action need to be made in each of these areas? Write them down. Be practical and start out with the ones you can achieve quickly. More important than writing them down, is *doing them*!

No matter how bad things may seem or how hopeless you may feel at times, you can always take positive, Decisive Actions. You'll never be "nowhere," and you'll never have absolutely "nothing." As long as you have breath in your lungs, there is something *you can do*. Remember the sign that hung above our kitchen door: "Do what you can, where you are, with what you have." Let this burn deep into your psyche. From now on, there are no excuses—you're a world-class winner!

Here's your next Decisive Action: Get ready for Step 4.

WIN*OLOGY* 101

STEP 1
URGENT EXCELLENCE

STEP 2
POSITIVE CONVICTION

STEP 3
DECISIVE ACTION

6

STEP 4:
MASTER YOUR CRAFT

Congratulations! You've already recognized opportunities and captured them. You've also begun to find the true positive in every situation and have taken Decisive Action to move forward to championship status. Now, the fun begins.

It's time to walk in WIN*ology* Step 4: Master Your Craft.

If you've ever heard the songs, "Because You Love Me," (Celine Dion); "Blue Eyes Blue," (Eric Clapton); "Unbreak My Heart," (Toni Braxton); or "I Don't Want to Miss a Thing," (Aerosmith), along with hundreds of other chart-topping hits, then you've heard the work of songwriter, Diane Warren. Her songs have received seven Academy Award nominations; five Golden Globe nominations, including one win (Best Original Song for the movie, *Burlesque*); and 12 Grammy Award nominations, including one win for "Because You Love Me." Without a doubt, Diane Warren is one of the most successful, highly sought-after songwriters of our time.

Ms. Warren has risen to such high acclaim due to two primary reasons—her talent and her work ethic. Concerning both, she said these words:

> *"You have to hone your craft, but you also have to be born with a certain amount of talent, and I never took the talent for granted—I've always worked really hard to be as good as I could be."*

Notice her last comment, "I've always worked really hard to be as good as I could be." I believe this is the mantra for every high-performing winner—including you!

We've come to the stage in WIN*ology* where it's time to Master Your Craft. Understand, your dream is different than everyone else's, and it might require a different level of education and specific skills. Regardless of your path or desired destination, striving to perpetually improve your game is a requirement to both get to the top *and* stay on top.

- THREE "FAVORITES" -

It's amazing how, throughout the course of your life, you hear so many sayings, quotes, and phrases. Some of them are very good and inspiring. Others? Well, let's just say they're flat-out ridiculous. Let me give you three of my "favorites" that you must never adhere to or believe on your road to greatness.

1. *"Knowledge is power."* We've heard this for so long, yet it's not the truth. Why? Mainly

Step 4: Master Your Craft

because it builds false hope. The truth is, knowledge, in and of itself, will not do you one bit of good in your quest for greatness. It's only when you *apply* the knowledge you've acquired that it turns into a valuable asset.

> **Acquiring knowledge isn't enough. Greatness comes by putting what you learn to work.**

Let's say my desire is to be a world-class pianist. (My mother would be so happy!) I could buy a stack of books on playing the piano; watch, "Learn to Play the Piano in 30 Days," on YouTube; and even observe and take notes from the greatest pianist in my area. Will all of this make me a great pianist? Absolutely not! My quest to greatness begins when I *apply* what I've learned. Oh, by the way, they call that "practicing!"

Acquiring knowledge isn't enough. Greatness comes by putting what you learn to work.

2. **"I'm doing the best I can."** Welcome to the war cry of mediocrity! In most occasions, this is really a code phrase for, "Don't expect me to do more than the bare minimum!" Actor

Sean Connery put it best in the movie, *The Rock*. With his thick Scottish brogue, he said, "Losers always whine about doing their best!" The same is true today . . . but not for WIN*ologists*. We are the ones who go above and beyond to be the best we can possibly be.

3. *"I might not be the sharpest tool in the shed."* Seriously? As if the world needs any more dull tools lying around! If, for some unknown reason, you're only going to be a "tool in the shed," at least train yourself to be a highly-tuned, surgical-grade instrument forged for a specific purpose. We already have enough old, rusty, worn out screwdrivers laying around!

I think you get the point.

To Master Your Craft will require a constant application of knowledge, going above and beyond what's "normal" or required, and the continual sharpening of your skill sets. Whether your goal is to be a world-class mom and housewife (which is very honorable and possibly the most challenging vocation of all), a top international investment banker, the chief of police in your city, a nationally-recognized school teacher, a fitness coach with a clientele list of the "Who's Who" in your region, or a professional athlete—you can never stop the pursuit to improve and Master Your Craft.

STEP 4: MASTER YOUR CRAFT

- GOOD OR GREAT -

The great Hungarian composer and pianist, Franz Liszt, revealed the power and significance of mastering his craft when he said:

"Miss one day of practice, I notice; miss two, the critics notice; miss three, the audience notices."

No matter how good you are now, you can always be better...

You can become great.

One of the very best business/motivational books written in the past 20 years is Jim Collins' *Good to Great*. His most famous line from this writing is simply, "Good is the enemy to great."[1] Collins is true with his sentiments; WIN*ologists* can never settle for just "good enough." Why? Because the second you do, you risk the beginning of your demise.

My favorite takeaway from reading Collins' classic was one simple question: What can I be the best in the world at? This incredible and probing inquiry is one I believe everyone must address, individually and corporately, to become the world-class winners we were born to be.

In the 2014 blockbuster movie, *Whiplash*, music conservatory professor, Terence Fletcher (played brilliantly by Academy Award winner, J.K. Simmons), has one mission—to build the best jazz music program in the world.[2] An inspiring young drummer, Andrew (played by

Miles Teller), joins the ensemble in hopes of making the cut. Little did he know how much Fletcher would push him to bring out his fullest potential.

In one captivating scene, Fletcher and Andrew are engaged in a conversation concerning what it takes to be the best in the world. With a glaze in his eyes and a look of disgust on his face, Fletcher leans over and tells young Andrew one of the most thought-provoking statements of the entire movie. He said:

> *"There are no two words any more harmful in the English language than, 'Good job.'"*

Think about this statement for a moment. How many people, when they hear these two words, believe they've "arrived?" To the masses, "good job" is a form of high praise; to the WIN*ologist*, they're a confirmation of the obvious: They haven't yet mastered their craft. More work still needs to be done. Music legend, Ray Charles, put his spin on this concept by saying:

> *"I never wanted to be famous. I only wanted to be great."*

At the highest level of my competition career, gold medals could literally be decided within fractions of a second or inch. Taekwondo isn't only a very physical art, the mental game is just as intense. Just like in a highly competitive chess match, one wrong move could completely shift the playing field. For example, in technical competitions—where the perfection of your form was judged—one lost second of concentration, the slightest bobble, or even the smallest error in posture could cost you the gold medal. If you wanted to win gold, "good" wasn't going to cut it.

You had to be great.

Becoming great, let alone the best in the world, sounds like a daunting task. It is; however, no one arrives at that plateau overnight. The good news is, you don't have to! American radio personality and respected human character development expert, Earl Nightingale, laid it out this way: "If you spend 30 minutes, every day, learning about one specific subject, you'll become a legitimate expert in six months."

Thirty minutes . . . every day . . . for six short months. That's all. Instead of watching your favorite sitcom or nightly news for the next six months, invest that time into your passion and watch it grow. I promise, the results will astound you. I put this to the test in 2010 by writing at least 30 minutes a day. The result? My first book published in 2011. Regardless of the magnitude of your dream, you start your journey by taking bite-sized daily steps. So, what are you waiting on?

Start today.

You can't settle for the "good job" level you've already attained. You must strive for constant and never-ending improvement. It really comes down to a few simple questions:

- Why settle for good when you can have great?
- Why settle for great when you can be superior?
- Why stop at superior when you can be world-class?

It all comes down to continuously mastering your craft.

- THE WINNER'S WAY -

In my specific field of martial arts, we adhered to and rigorously trained in a philosophy called Choong Sil. In fact, the Grand Masters of the progressive combat Taekwondo style, in which I am trained, referred to our sect as Choong Sil Kwan: The way of constant and never-ending improvement. This philosophy became more than a way of fighting for me; it became a building block for my life and a component of all my successes. Now, it can become the same foundation for you.

Let's call it, "The Winner's Way."

What exactly is The Winner's Way? Fundamentally, it's a mindset which provokes you forward to greatness. For me, it translated into a quest for excellence. Two components play a vital role in this type of lifestyle: critique and motivation.

I don't know about you, but I've never met anyone who likes to be critiqued. It goes against our human need for acceptance and recognition. But, too much acceptance

STEP 4: MASTER YOUR CRAFT

and "Attaboys" can prove to be destructive to our performance. Critiques hurt mainly because after you've done your best, you still have a list of areas to improve. As difficult as it is, *not* "facing the music" will obstruct your path to greatness and greatly limit your chances for victory.

The way of a winner is a life full of constant, never-ending improvement.

No matter where I found myself on the "good" meter, I knew there was always room for improvement. So, I learned to live a life open to constant, honest critique in which everything about me was evaluated. Embracing this one principle changed my life forever.

Along with honest critique, undying motivation is another facet of The Winner's Way.

Part of the Global Taekwondo Federation U.S. national team's daily ritual included spending hours upon hours on routines and fighting combinations. Our weekend training camps, especially those leading up to international events, included three, two-to-three-hour, grueling training sessions, with only a short break for lunch and dinner inbetween. The level of pain was unbearable at times, but the hope for the gold pulled us like a ten-ton magnet to victory.

As you begin to Master Your Craft, ask yourself, "What's my gravitational pull to the gold?" What motivates you and pulls you forward through tough times? If your goals are vocational, maybe it's a performance bonus, a promotion, a raise, or the opportunity for ownership/partnership. If they're educational, perhaps an award, a degree, a certification, or an internship is your pulling force. While these types of goals are easier to define, as they're attached to rewards, others are harder to distinguish.

Goals connected to health, parenting, relationships, or hobbies can carry a much more difficult definition of reward. Thus, motivation can run thin at times. To keep moving forward in the mastery of these areas, you may find yourself creating your own rewards. For example, treat yourself to a spa day, a weekend trip, or shopping spree when you accomplish victories along the way. No matter how you create your "gravitational gold," keep moving forward and keep focused on your desired future. It's The Winner's Way—and winning is fun!

-The Evolution of Mastering-

Remember the WIN*ology* 101 scientific process? Let's revisit it for a moment and then tie it to Step 4: Master Your Craft.

> **Imitation.** As stated earlier, mastering your craft is about gaining knowledge and then applying that knowledge to what you already know. If your quest is to be the best in the world (and I know it is), then find those who are the best, right now, in the space you desire to occupy. Then, ask yourself a few questions:

Step 4: Master Your Craft

- What do they do that makes them the best?
- How did they arrive at their status?
- What obstacles did they overcome?
- What mistakes did they make and what lessons did they learn from them?

Never feel like it's a slap in the face to learn from "the greats." Imitate first—even at this level of your journey.

Innovation. After you've perfected *Imitation* at this level, then comes *Innovation*. This is where honing your craft becomes fun and tremendously invigorating. It's where you begin to "feel the music," so to speak.

During this phase, you begin to move away from the physical and mechanical side of mastering your craft into the soulful and spiritual side. Consequently, you become more reflexive and natural as opposed to robotic and forced. *Innovation* is the artistic phase where your creative juices begin to flow, producing results that are more effortless and natural. No longer are you imitating the sounds of others; you're now making your own music.

Inspiration. The more you improve your craft, the more you become a modern-day warrior poet—powerful and inspired. Now, instead of coloring by the numbers, the paint brush of your craft flows with ease and is blown by the wind of creativity and *Inspiration*.

By looking at the etymology of the word "inspire"—a combination of the two words "in" and "spirit"—you quickly come to realize this truth: Winning can be spiritual. Mastering your craft releases tremendous *Inspiration* as you connect with your inner soul and spirit, as well as the Divine. At this point, you begin to realize something that you might not have ever experienced up until now: *This is what you were born to do!*

There's no better feeling in this world.

Identification. As you have studied, trained, practiced, and performed, your craft is now instinctual. With your skill sets now functioning at their maximum capacity, your entire way of thinking has changed. You're beginning to see you and your craft through a different lens: winning. You expect it, plan for it, and have mapped it out in your five-, 10-, and 15-year goals. This is your present and your future.

The winner you were created to be is now being unleashed. Your personal evolution has uncovered the potential that always lay deep within you

Welcome to your new identity.

What made Steve Jobs, Bill Gates, and Michael Dell modern legends of personal computing? Were they just

Step 4: Master Your Craft

smarter than everyone else? Obviously, they each possess(ed) a great deal of intelligence and talent, but talent alone—though a prerequisite for greatness—wasn't enough. Their success is a result of their own "secret sauce" of these four phases, coupled with the tenacity to constantly master their craft. Their results?

They became the greatest at the highest level in their field.

- Stay with It -

As we close Step 4, let's tackle first things first: your WIN*ology* Assignments for this stage.

STEP 4
- Master Your Craft -
Assignments

- Spend a minimum of 30 minutes every day, developing and mastering your craft.
- Identify the areas of your natural giftedness in which you can be the best in the world.

- Make a list of the skill sets you already possess.
- Make a list of the next skills you're determined to master and become an expert in.
- Create a training plan; specifically, how you will master these areas of your craft.

Maybe you're winning in some areas of your life at the highest levels, yet feel like you're losing big in others. That's okay. It's actually totally natural. WIN*ology* is a philosophical process designed to translate throughout all the facets of your life. Remember, this isn't a quick fix, but a step-by-step system designed to propel you into your destiny as a world-class winner . . . and then keep you there.

And that's exactly where we're going next. The following section of this book holds the secrets of how to stay on top.

WIN*OLOGY* 101

STEP 1
URGENT EXCELLENCE

STEP 2
POSITIVE CONVICTION

STEP 3
DECISIVE ACTION

STEP 4
MASTER YOUR CRAFT

7

STEP 5:
PLAYING INBOUNDS

What do the former world's number one golfer, Tiger Woods; former world heavyweight boxing champion, Mike Tyson; former A-list actress, Lindsay Lohan; epic Hollywood sweetheart, Judy Garland; former world's best-selling pop artist, Britney Spears; former U.S. president, Bill Clinton; former congressman, Anthony Weiner; and former nightly news anchor, Brian Williams, all have in common? (Besides the "former" part, that is.) All these former greats—and a laundry list of others too long to mention—had major ethical scandals. They all have something else in common, as well: Not one of them "fell from grace" due to their lack of talent, but rather from their lack of integrity.

While they had mastered their specific craft and were reaping the accompanying benefits, each one failed to remain at the top of their field, because they didn't play inbounds.

Welcome to your next step of WIN*ology*, where it's all

about staying on top. How do you accomplish such a task? One way is obvious: You must stay inbounds.

- Play by the Rules -

Let's take a quick test. Try to name a sport or game where staying inbounds isn't part of the competition. Go ahead, think of one. You probably can't do it. Even if you could think up one, you might need an ice pack and some Advil to quell your headache after finally finding some obscure example!

From checkers and chess to basketball, baseball, football, boxing, ice hockey, even Ping-Pong, Foursquare, and Uno—rules and boundaries are a part of every game. In soccer, if the ball goes out of bounds, you forfeit your possession. In football, step out of bounds and the play is dead or you become ineligible. If you stray from the course during a marathon, you're disqualified from winning.

You don't have to be an avid sports fan to realize this one fact: If you don't play inbounds, you can't win. Period.

Much like sports, the game of life has the exact same setup. If you go out of bounds or don't play by the rules, you lose. Sadly, our world is full of real-life examples.

It's almost impossible to watch the news and not see another personal, ethical, or moral scandal being revealed. From Hollywood to D.C., the rate at which "winners" derail and self-destruct is at epidemic proportions. Why is this pattern so rampant? It's quite simple: Even though these life-champions mastered their crafts exceptionally well, they refused to play within the boundaries in other parts of their lives. Through infidelity, drug abuse, financial misconduct, criminal activity, or behavior unbefitting of their office/position, many "greats" have imploded their own future and lost the crown they once donned.

Please, don't take this as a cheap, critical shot at those who have been marked by their mistakes. I'm as frail and prone to mistakes as any man. My intention isn't to judge anyone, but merely to examine the patterns so we can all learn from the errors of others and avoid making them ourselves. I would never discredit anyone with such great achievements. Personally, I have enormous respect for what they have accomplished and hope they one day rebound to greatness. This chapter is about simply making a sobering point:

> ***Remaining a winner can prove to be a greater challenge than becoming a winner.***

To remain on top, you must set and live within boundaries.

- THE WORD NO ONE LIKES -

Let's face it. Just to mention the word "boundaries" can send shivers down your spine. Why is this? It stems from childhood. From infancy, no one likes to be told, "No." We don't even like to tell ourselves, "No!" But boundaries, in and of themselves, aren't all bad. It really comes down to how you perceive them. Are boundaries set in place to restrict you from having fun, or are they the mechanism to keep you in check and on top? How you view them makes all the difference.

Boundaries are applicable and beneficial to every part of our lives—our time, our money, our relationships, etc. I learned this when a mentor once told me, "Joel, if you don't set your own schedule, someone else will set it for you." That's all I needed to hear. I knew some boundaries concerning my time had to be set in place.

> **Winning in life is fun, but if you play outside the boundaries, you do so at your own risk.**

From that moment forward, I began to intentionalize my schedule and fit others inside my boundary. No more run here, run there, go cater to this person on a whim, take this call during family dinner, etc. Over the years, this simple discipline has helped me maintain a balance between my personal and professional lives. Believe me, for my personality, it's been hard at times. But in the end, living within this one boundary has kept my family and faith in proper priority and health.

Life is a game, but sometimes it can be cruel. Winning in life is fun, but if you play outside the boundaries, you do so at your own risk.

Step 5: Playing Inbounds

For example, if you break the boundaries of your marriage, you stand the high risk of losing your marriage and family. Even if you somehow stay married, the breach of trust is, at times, impossible to repair.

When doctors step outside the lines of their medical oaths, they stand the risk of losing their license and practice.

> **Failure to practice and exude self-control in the private areas of our lives can and will result in loss of control in the public areas.**

Break the boundaries of your business or financial responsibilities, and you may find yourself in bankruptcy court.

How do you play inbounds? What's the secret to staying within the parameters established for your success? One way to ensure you play by the rules is by activating self-control.

No one is exempt from the destruction connected to a lack of self-control. No one. Failure to consistently practice and exude self-control in the private areas of our lives can and will result in a loss of control in our public lives. In the words of renowned author, A.R. Bernard:

> *"Your gifts and abilities may take you where your character cannot sustain you."*

This staggering reality should jolt us into a moment of reflection. If it happened to these (and other) former greats, could it happen to anyone?

Undoubtedly.

All of us have a loved one, relative, co-worker, or dear friend who we've painfully watched collapse due to severe self-indulgence or a basic lack of self-control. Yet, we live in an age that is quick to offer pacified "justification" for such calamities. Be it "a mid-life crisis" or "I just had to get it out of my system," or even, "I never thought I'd get caught," excuses for poor judgment are widespread. Still, many choose to roll the dice, betting they will be the one who walks away unscathed.

- STAY IN THE RING-

In the summer of 1997, I found myself in the fight of my life. It was day three of the Global Taekwondo Federation World Championships, and I was in the middleweight division's gold medal round. The world championship was on the line and within my grasp.

The tournament had been one of the most taxing I had ever participated in. Phase 1 was strewn with injuries: broken hands, broken noses, and broken ribs, just to name a few. Now the cream of the competition was rising to the top. The world's best fighters and technicians were all ready to lay it on the line for victory. Thankfully, I was one of them.

Surviving through 40 of the best middle-weight fight-

Step 5: Playing Inbounds

ers in the world wasn't easy, especially since I was dealing with several injuries myself. My strategy, savvy, and experience had kept me alive thus far, but the gold medal match would prove to be the toughest of my career. Preparation and prelims were over; it was time for the big show.

My opponent was the reigning Norwegian national champion, Per Jonny. Even though we shared the same weight class, Per Jonny was easily a foot taller than me. (I always wondered how he made it into the middle-weight division.) Overall, the Norwegian national team was one of the best in the federation, with fighters who were experts at winning. Per Jonny was Norway's best.

From the beginning of the fight, I felt as though I was losing. Per Jonny's superior height meant that he could hit me from a mile away, which he did quite often. To make matters worse, Per Jonny was quite the Norwegian showman—celebrating and working the crowd (along with the judges) with every punch he landed. His theatrics were like rubbing salt in my wounds, . . . but it didn't last for long.

Somewhere in the midst of our bout, something happened to me. I reached the point where I just couldn't take it anymore. Like "Squints" Palledorous in the movie, *The Sandlot*, I snapped. Per Jonny had no idea what was about to happen—and neither did I.

In my entire fighting career, never could I remember a match where I completely lost it . . . until now. Like a crossbreed between an Army Blackhawk helicopter and

The Tasmanian Devil, I threw myself at the big Norwegian with no holds barred. I unleashed a flurry of moves, the last of which I buried my fist deep into Jonny's chin. THUMP! Just like that, he was down for the count. There was only one problem...

This wasn't a full contact event!

As expert martial artists, part of the mastery of our art form is to display utmost control and composure at all times. Never were we to show anger or a loss of control. Although we were fighting at full speed and power, the beauty of the sport was to control our moves to where we could stop on a dime if need be. The whole idea was to "own" your opponents while still honoring them and not intentionally causing debilitating bodily damage.

This all sounds good in theory, but for testosterone-filled, elite fighters in our twenties, it was a struggle at times. Unfortunately, on this occasion, I fell prey to the struggle.

After my barrage of kicks and punches, it seemed as though Jonny's body fell to the mat in super slow motion. Even as he was going down, I knew I was in trouble. I'll never forget the look in Coach Rob's eyes. He knew I had potentially thrown away my chances at the world middleweight title—all due to a brief moment of losing my cool.

My infraction was an excessive contact foul (You think?), which carried a loss of four points. Although I was still in the fight, losing four points from the scorecard was a dagger in the heart of my gold medal dreams. Not only was I being outscored, but now I had to overcome a four-point deficit.

STEP 5: PLAYING INBOUNDS

Without a doubt, I had broken a boundary, but the fight wasn't over. Jonny was allowed to recover. My resolve was, for the remaining two rounds, to push Jonny even harder. And that's exactly what I did. Through the physical pain and mental anguish that I'd thrown away my chances, I pushed. Over and over, my onslaught of attacks pushed Jonny outside the lines of the ring. Little did I realize how this would eventually work in my favor.

Finally, the fight was over. A new champion was about to be crowned. My body hurt all over, but even worse, my mind and emotions were playing havoc on me, over my uncontrolled lashout. With the referee holding both of our hands—one which would be lifted, declaring the new world champion—the announcer proclaimed the official decision: "The winner and middle-class world champion . . . Joel Scrivner, Team USA!"

I was ecstatic; Jonny was in complete shock.

How had this happened? Watching the playback revealed how Per Jonny lost, and I won. In the end, he had technically outscored me; however, whenever he was out of bounds, his scoring did not count. That element, combined with the fact that I controlled the ring and the pace of the fight—forcing him out of bounds 12 times—resulted in him losing 12 points! Yes, we were both world-class fighters, but Playing Inbounds was the difference between winning and losing.

Recovering from my brief lack of control and regaining my sense of boundaries secured me the gold medal and the title as the world champion. I went on to win five medals at that meet, including three gold-medal world championship titles. The medals were great, but the lesson I learned that day was far more valuable:

If you want to win, you have to play inbounds.

- THE "A" WORD -

While the first few chapters of this book have been speckled with a few words you might find uncomfortable (or repulsive), I have some news for you: The speckling isn't quite over! Welcome to the dreaded "A" word of WIN*ology*: accountability.

> We were both world-class fighters, but Playing Inbounds was the difference between winning and losing.

Earlier in this chapter, I said that no one is immune from the temptation of playing out of bounds. It's the truth. One of the best ways you can stave off temptation and protect against derailment is through accountability. Not only is it a great way to stay inbounds, it's also a masterful way to grow and develop in your life and skills. But the opposite is true, as well.

I once heard someone I *used* to respect say, "Man, accountability is bull! I just tell people whatever they want to hear. It doesn't actually do a thing." Obviously, this man

Step 5: Playing Inbounds

wasn't . . . and isn't . . . and probably never will be a WIN*ologist*. In fact, in the months following his ignorant words, his arrogance, and lust to continually play out of bounds painfully destroyed his life, family, career, respect, influence, finances, friendships, and future. I've often wondered how different his life could have been by incorporating this simple WIN*ology* principle: Play by the rules and have strong accountability.

I may never know.

What I do know is that strong accountability is essential for winning. If my coach had not reined me in when I derailed in the gold medal round, I would've never regained my composure and won the match. It was my coach's strong leadership, and especially my submission to his leadership, which allowed me to believe there was still hope and time left to re-establish my game plan. His commitment to hold me accountable to what I knew to do was the difference between winning and losing.

The benefits of accountability aren't new. In fact, this word has been thrown around in many circles for years. I know for my life, especially during the most daunting years, accountability has been more than just a trendy buzz word—it's been a lifesaver.

So, the question to ask yourself is: "Who can I be accountable to?" That's not easy to answer. Finding the right person can be difficult, but it's a requirement for winning.

Start by looking at the people currently in your life. Look hard. Who are your partners, coaches, teammates, and true friends—the ones who don't pull any punches, nor do they only tell you what you want to hear. Don't freak out, but . . . (Don't you hate it when people tell you not to freak out?) If you're struggling to come up with at least one, your future potential is greatly limited. Simply put, you cannot become, or remain, a world-class winner all by yourself. As a WIN*ologist*, finding strategic accountability partners must be a top priority if you desire to win in life at the highest levels.

One of our nation's founding fathers, Thomas Paine, once said:

"A body of men holding themselves accountable to nobody ought not to be trusted by anybody."

Yes, you can live a double life that no one knows about, slack off from your responsibilities, and resist the challenges of valuable accountability partners, but doing so positions you for disaster. I can tell you from experience, this is not the way of champions. Champions submit themselves to great coaches, faithful teammates, and credible voices in their lives. Why? Because they know how important it is to stay inbounds on all fronts in order to ensure future victories.

The same will be true for you and your success. Don't fear the dreaded "A" word. Much like boundaries, accountability isn't a tool to ruin your life. In fact, it very well could save it.

Step 5: Playing Inbounds

– Stay a Winner –

Hear me very clearly: While it's one thing to arrive at the top of your specific gift, talent, or craft, it's a whole different enchilada to stay there. Not only will your haters and competition—some as equally talented and more determined—be looking to knock you out, you can also self-destruct, leaving your position open game to the next person in line. The good news is you can stay on top, if you're willing to play inbounds, exercise self-control, and depend on accountability partners to help you stay on course.

Let's set the record straight. It's not always the short skirt or Mr. "Tall, Dark, and Handsome" who destroys households, finances, and vocations. Sometimes healthy pursuits, taken completely out of bounds, cause the most damage.

I've watched people, who were sexually faithful to their spouse, destroy their marriage because of an inconspicuous "other woman": work and ambition. Other people have sacrificed their family on the altar of their obsessions with hobbies or physical training goals. And let's not forget the root of all evil—the love of money. Many a family, fortune, or futures have been slain over the relentless pursuit of the almighty dollar. (Just watch a few episodes of CNBC's hit show, *American Greed*.)

So, what are the areas in your life where you're most prone to step out of bounds? Is it over spending? Partying? Carousing? Flirting? Eating? Cheating? Lying? Relaxing? Working? Truly, anything moved outside of healthy boundaries can destroy what you hold dear. Moderation in all things is the best M.O.

With this in mind, here are your WIN*ology* Assignments for Step 5: Playing Inbounds:

STEP 5
- PLAYING INBOUNDS -
ASSIGNMENTS

- Take an honest assessment of your potential danger areas. Where could you most likely derail?

- In what areas of your life are you currently activating self-control? Are there some areas where you need to exercise more self-control? Write them down.

- Find accountability partners—true friends with whom who you can share these areas and set up safeguards and boundaries.

- Set up regular meetings or phone calls with your accountability partners to discuss progress and any potential weaknesses. If you sense danger, reach out. The best in the world have blown it, so don't kid yourself. Honesty is always the best policy and confession is good for the soul.

Step 5: Playing Inbounds

This is no joke. Taking action on this WIN*ology* step can protect and save your life, professionally and personally.

WIN*ology* is about building a lifetime of winning and a legacy of victory. It's not enough to get on top; you must do everything you can to stay on top. I like to say it like this: "If you're ever going to be known as a 'former' anything, let it be due to the fact that you moved on to bigger and better—or you died!"

Winning now and for years to come is your identity. It's who you are and what you do. But to be on top and to hold that position, Playing Inbounds is a must.

WIN*OLOGY* 101

STEP 1
URGENT EXCELLENCE

STEP 2
POSITIVE CONVICTION

STEP 3
DECISIVE ACTION

STEP 4
MASTER YOUR CRAFT

STEP 5
PLAYING INBOUNDS

8

STEP 6:
TENACIOUS ENDURANCE

The WIN*ology* journey has taken us into many components comprising *The Evolution of Winning*: a science, an art form, a renewed state of mind, and an identity, just to name a few. Now, let's explore what WIN*ology* is not:

WIN*ology* is *not* a feeling.

Sure, winning feels good. In fact, it feels great! But while we love the feeling, winning cannot be obtained simply on feelings or emotions. Winning (as discussed in Step 3) is a decision. Not only must you choose to do whatever it takes to win—legally, ethically, and morally—you must also dedicate yourself to the essential sixth step of WIN*ology* to continue your pursuit of winning.

You must develop Tenacious Endurance.

- All the Way -

1968. Olympic stadium, Mexico City.

The crowd stood and roared with excitement as the 1968 Olympic Men's Marathon came to a close. Shortly after the race was completed, Mamo Wolde from Ethiopia, Kenji Kimihara from Japan, and New Zealand's Mike Ryan, took the gold, silver, and bronze medal stands, respectively. But they weren't the only winners that day. In fact, there was another champion—an unsung hero—who might have been an even greater champion in his own right.

Tanzanian, John Stephen Akhwari.

Akhwari fought seemingly insurmountable obstacles the entire race. Not long after the starting gun fired, he began to experience severe cramps due to the high altitude in which he had never trained. About half-way through the race, as runners began to jockey for position, Akhwari was knocked hard to the ground, dislocating his knee and injuring his shoulder on the hard surface.

Still, he continued.

Over an hour after three men stood on the winner's podiums, their hearts beating with national pride as they watched their flags being raised, another champion entered the practically empty stadium. There were no cameras, no fanfare, and no roar of the crowd. The only thing left was one man's inward drive.

Battered and torn, John Stephen Akhwari stumbled around the Olympic stadium track, now lit by lights as the sun had long set. Twenty-five miles completed left only

Step 6: Tenacious Endurance

one mile to go—four laps around the stadium's track. One lap, two laps, three laps, and then the fourth and final lap. Crossing the finish line, Akhwari was met by a small group of reporters who had received word of his heroism. When asked why he did it, the champion who no one saw, said these riveting words:

> **"My country did not send me 5,000 miles to start this race; they sent me 5,000 miles to finish this race."**

And finish he did. Akhwari endured to the end—the mark of a true WIN*ologist*.

- Keep Your Cool -

Tenacious Endurance spans the range of human existence. Take the animal kingdom as an example—in particular, the camel. Able to traverse thousands of miles while storing water in its humps, the camel can survive six to seven months, depending on the time of year, without drinking a drop of water. Most of us learned of the camel's amazing internal hydration system in grade school, but there's a powerful, yet lesser known physiological phenomenon found in our humpback friends.

Not only is the camel a walking oasis, it functions as a portable central air-conditioning unit, as well—fluctuating its internal core temperature by up to 12 degrees Fahrenheit. Essentially, when it's hot outside, the camel can reduce the heat inside its own body. But that's not all. The camel's brain is an amazing work of science, as well.

While the camel's body is cooling down, its brain has the ability to operate a separate internal cooling system. This enables the camel's brain to remain cooler than its core temperature. In doing so, it can continue to function at the highest levels of efficiency, even in the most extreme climate environments. When it's all said and done, you could reasonably deduct that one of the ways camels demonstrate Tenacious Endurance is by keeping a cool head!

Now, let's take "CAMELology," break it down, and then apply it to WIN*ology*.

How many times have you fallen victim to fatigue, simply due to your inability to keep a cool head? Everybody has. When things begin to heat up on the outside, we tend to allow our external surroundings to negatively affect us inside. Our emotions begin to boil, causing us to lose control. In other words, we get hot-headed.

> **WIN***ologists* **must learn how to hold it together from the inside out.**

We all know a hot-head—someone who is the first to blow their top and lose their cool, sometimes over miniscule issues. However, dealing with pressure and enduring hard times isn't just about your external conditioning; it also encompasses your internal conditioning. The truth is, you need to learn to keep a cool

Step 6: Tenacious Endurance

head even in the midst of volatile situations.

Baseball legend, Lou Gehrig said:

> *"The ballplayer who loses his head, who can't keep his cool is worse than no ball player at all."*

Keep your cool. Stay in the game. You've got a lot more winning ahead.

Enduring through hard times is tough; however, there are a number of tools which can help you stay cool, even in the midst of the battle. Prayer, meditation, positive internal dialogue, deep breathing techniques, are just a few. I do all the above.

Whatever it takes for you to keep a cool head in heated situations, do it. Remember your Positive Conviction and your new, true, positive realities learned in Step 2? When faced with circumstances that challenge your perception and threaten to turn positivity into negativity, pull out your journal and start reading your new, true, positive declarations. It might sound crazy, but believe me; it works! By meditating on those positive declarations, you literally reprogram your brain and greatly reduce the power of current negative circumstances. With a cool head, you can better navigate through negative situations to a positive solution.

Like many other WIN*ology* steps, Tenacious Endurance isn't easy to master. One of the secrets, however, is learning to control your emotions and feelings and continuing to do the right things for the right reasons. When you do, you can make it through the longest of seasons, in the hottest conditions, without one drink of water, so to speak.

WIN*ologists* must learn how to hold it together from the inside out. Whether it's sinking the tricky, four-foot putt to win lunch, negotiating with a stubborn three year-old at the dinner table; selecting the correct phrase to calm a frustrated, venting spouse; or overcoming an objection to close the biggest deal of your career—your ability to be patient, calm, and poised will set you up to win!

- What Winners Never Do -

No one arrives at the highest political offices in the land without Tenacious Endurance. One of Britain's greatest statesmen, and former Prime Minister of the U.K., Sir Winston Churchill, knew firsthand this voyage. In one of his most famous speeches, he gave the world his success secret when he said:

"Never, never, never, never give up."

Sir Winston was a master of Tenacious Endurance. He inspired nations with other notable statements such as, "If you're going through hell, keep going!" and, "Success is the ability to go from failure to failure without losing enthusiasm."

Step 6: Tenacious Endurance

So, what do winners never do? It's simple: They never, ever give up.

Contrary to popular belief, winners don't always win. Winners suffer losses and setbacks just like everyone else in life. The difference is this: Winners never quit. If you don't believe me, then look at a few winners who were, at one time in their life, considered miserable losers.

Henry Ford. Known around the world as the grandfather of the automobile industry, Ford failed numerous times on his way to the top of his field. His first venture to build a motor car dissolved after only a year and a half, mainly due to stockholder confidence (or the lack thereof). Ford rallied enough money to start again, only to have his second venture fold, as well. Despite the fact that almost the entire motor industry had lost faith in him, Ford never quit. And the rest is history.

Walt Disney. One of the world's greatest film and entertainment icons didn't start out that way. Walt Disney was fired from his first job at the Kansas City Star Newspaper because he "lacked creativity." His first business, Laugh-O-Gram, launched in 1922, which produced cartoons and short advertising films. Less than 18 months after inception, Disney filed for bankruptcy. Not to be denied, Walt Disney packed up and fled the Midwest to Hollywood, CA, where he would start the Walt Disney Company. As of May 2015, Disney's company employs 180,000 worldwide and is valued by Forbes as the 11th most valuable brand at $179.5 billion.

Richard Branson. Billionaire Richard Branson's name is attached to several multi-million-dollar brands including Virgin Air, Virgin Atlantic, Virgin Music, and Virgin Active. However, this dyslexic, 16 year-old, high school dropout didn't start on top. On his last day at school, Richard's headmaster told him he would either end up in prison or a millionaire. Richard chose the latter. Based out of a church and using his floundering student magazine, *The Student*, to advertise, young Richard started selling music records. Richard chose the name, Virgin, for his record business because that's what he was: a "virgin" in business. Branson's mail-order business exploded to the point where he eventually opened his first store, Virgin Records, on Oxford Street in London. Today, Branson, worth $5.1 billion, is potentially Britain's highest profile billionaire and considered one of the wealthiest men in the world.

J.K. Rowling. "It's far too long for a children's book," and, "Children's books never make money," were the comments heard all too often by author, J.K. Rowling, as publisher after publisher refused her manuscript. Still, the divorced mom, living on welfare, pursued her dream of having her series published and sold. Finally, her tenacity paid off. The Harry Potter series has sold over 400 million

STEP 6: TENACIOUS ENDURANCE

copies, making it one of the most successful and lucrative book and film series of all time. Somebody was wrong—this children's book made Rowling (and her publisher) a fortune.

History is full of stories just like these. Steve Jobs was once fired from Apple, the company he would eventually lead into world-class renown. Donald Trump also struggled on numerous occasions before making billions in commercial real estate. Bill Gates, Oprah Winfrey, Wayne Huizenga, H.J. Heinz, Milton Hershey, and many others all endured hardship and failure, yet they endured to find success and untold riches. How did they do it? They never quit. Why? I'll tell you why: because quitting is the number one way to guarantee a loss.

> **World-class winners . . . refuse to be overwhelmed by what they *can't do* and focus on what they *can do*.**

- THE WINNING DIFFERENCE -

John Wooden, one of the most revered coaches in NCAA history, leading his UCLA Bruins basketball team to an unprecedented record with 10 national championships in 12 years, gave these words of advice concerning success and failure:

> *"Success is never final, failure is never fatal. It's courage that counts."*

The difference between failure and success? Courage, mixed with the tenacity to endure.

Almost every child, somewhere in their life, has heard the famous saying, "Winners never quit and quitters never win." My parents not only instilled this into me at a young age, they actually went a few steps further. They took Decisive Action.

In the Scrivner house, there was a simple rule us kids had to follow. We were never allowed to quit—at anything!

I remember the day I decided to play the piano. My parents agreed, but with a small stipulation. Knowing the cost and time commitment involved in learning how to play the piano, they made me sign a one-year contract. I couldn't quit—at least for one year. Did I want to quit? Of course I did, probably about a month into the deal. But, I had to stick it out all the way till the end.

I'm glad I did.

This value system, in- stilled in me at a young age, would last my entire life. During my fighting career, there were plenty of times where I felt mistreated, overlooked, or snubbed by a coach. But by then, my parents' ideology was so ingrained in me, quitting was never even an option in my mind. I had to endure and finish. In the end—while others came and went, came and went, came and went—I stuck it out. Was I always the best fighter in my group,

Step 6: Tenacious Endurance

school, or class? Probably not, but Tenacious Endurance became a basic instinct, differentiating me from my peers.

I had a college friend (We'll call him, "Rob.") who was undoubtedly one of the most talented individuals I had ever met. I mean, he was good at anything he touched. Darts, pool, football, girls, interviews, presentations—you name it, Rob was amazing at it. Actually, he was so good at so many things, it was often infuriating. Oh, and it didn't hurt that he was 6'2", strikingly good looking, and carried a "90's Alec Baldwin" swagger. Rob had it going on.

But Rob, although he "won" often, wasn't a true winner.

Rob arrived at college two years before me. Every semester, he loaded up his schedule with as many classes as the school would allow. (His parents footing the hefty price tag, of course.) But without fail, every semester was a sad repeat of the previous one. You see, Rob never finished one class—not one. He systematically dropped every single class by the assigned drop date, thus keeping his transcript free of any "F"s. But Rob's logic was faulty. Though his transcript never showed a failing grade, it also lacked something else vitally important: any actual college credits!

After three years of study, I had earned over 70 credit hours and my associate's degree, all while working full-time running my own business and paying cash for my own education. I received excellent marks and never dropped a single class even though the pressure to do so was great at times. The Tenacious Endurance I learned from my parents paid off. At the time I transitioned, Rob still hadn't completed a single class . . . in five years.

Rob was good at everything, but great at nothing. What he possessed in talent, he lacked in character. Like many people, he was a great starter but a horrible finisher. World-class winners are just the opposite. They refuse to be overwhelmed by what they *can't do* and focus on what they *can do*.

And, they finish what they start!

- STICK-TO-IT-IV-NESS -

Little did I know the invaluable lessons I had learned in my childhood would translate into my own parenting techniques. Today, I routinely hear myself telling my girls (much to their chagrin, I might add), "You're a Scrivner. Let's go! Finish strong! Scrivner's never quit!" As far as our girls are concerned, winning is in our blood and quitting is not an option.

One day while on a timed, one-mile run with my then 10 year-old daughter, Sydney, I was "encouraging" her with my patented "Scrivner's never quit" speech. In her usual quick wit, she quipped at my chiding, "Dad, 'Scrivner' means, *writer*; it doesn't mean, *don't quit*." Without hesitation, I responded, "Well, Sydney, if writers quit, then they'll never get anything written. Writers are finishers. So, Scrivner's never quit! Now, let's go!"

That day she set a new personal record in the one-mile run. (You're welcome, Sydney!)

Legendary inventor and American inspiration, Thomas Edison, made this amazing declaration:

STEP 6: TENACIOUS ENDURANCE

"Many of life's failures are experienced by people who did not realize how close they were to success when they gave up."

This statement is so painfully true.

Edison attributed his greatest achievements to common sense, hard work, and a word he also invented, "stick-to-it-iv-ness." Now it's one thing to invent a movie camera, incandescent lighting, and the first alkaline storage battery (just some of Edison's many inventions), but to create a word? That's greatness personified!

Stick-to-it-iv-ness is basically sticking it out when everything around you says to cut your losses and quit. In other words, it's Tenacious Endurance—the quality every WIN-*ologist* must adhere to and practice.

Many years ago, my friend, Ryan, talked me into training for a full, 26.2-mile marathon. (The last .2 is the hardest part.) The thought had never really entered my mind, mainly because I'm not into needless suffering. Also, my natural build is short and thick, not the Kenyan-esque frame of most long-distance runners. Nevertheless, I accepted the challenge.

One of the motivating factors in believing I could actually accomplish this maddening challenge was because of another long-time friend, Ralph. Now, Ralph was shorter, fatter (at the time), and much hairier than I was—none of which lend themselves to aerodynamic distance running. I'm embarrassed to admit that my own internal dialogue went something like this: "If this short, fat, hairy little monkey can do this, then what's my excuse? I'm a stinkin' world champion!"

(Hey, inspiration is found wherever it's found; mine just happened to be at the expense of my good friend! Ralph is still my friend to this day, . . . and his number is still saved in my cell phone under his pseudonym: Hairy Little Monkey.)

Full of myself and my new-found obnoxiously-negative inspiration, I began my daily torture sessions . . . I mean, training sessions.

Training for world championship titles was one thing, but nothing—I mean, absolutely nothing—could have prepared me for what Ryan talked me into! Within the first week, I felt as though my lungs were going to burst, my legs were on fire, and my heart was going to explode at any given moment. Telling him, "Man, I'm just too busy right now to commit to this," sounded better and better each day, but no . . . I'm a Scrivner; and Scrivner's . . . . You can finish the line!

I was determined, come hell or high water, to finish my training and run this marathon, even if it killed me. Many times, it felt as though it would.

From that day until now, I have trained and completed three, 26.2-mile marathons. In each race, one thing that blew me away was how many thousands of marathoners *didn't* have that Kenyan running physique, I so greatly coveted. In fact, I was surrounded by big people, little people; physically-challenged people, who were totally unfazed by their physical limitations; and countless senior

Step 6: Tenacious Endurance

citizens—all winners in my book. Their greatest exercise wasn't training their bodies; it was exercising massive amounts of mental stick-to-it-iv-ness as they prepared.

And as they did, they never gave up.

- Humble Pie -

One of my biggest "aha" moments came at mile 22 during my most recent marathon, held in Asheville, NC. As I struggled to ascend a steep hill, my jaw literally dropped when I was overtaken by a sweet, cute, little Asian grandmother who effortlessly ran past me! Of course, you better believe the internal trash talk quickly commenced.

"Where do you think you're going, Grandma? Oh, yeah, it's on now, sister! I'm coming for you! I'm gonna fly past you so fast, your head's gonna spin!"

Just then, Grandma found another gear and left me in the dust! No matter how hard I tried, I couldn't catch her. In fact, I tried so hard, I injured my Achilles' tendon which required four months of rehab. The truth is, much like Bob Barker took it to Adam Sandler in the movie, *Happy Gilmore*, Grandma kicked my butt!

And I'll never forget it.

But guess what? Even after being humiliated by a lady 20 to 30 years older than me and with my Achilles' tendon feeling like it had disengaged from my body, I didn't quit. I finished that marathon limping the last three miles. At the end of the race, I desperately needed two things: an ice pack for my leg and a big, cold drink to wash down the huge slice of humble pie I had just eaten!

- THE GOOD STUFF -

The lessons I've learned since the day Hairy Little Monkey inspired me to train and run a marathon have been countless. One of the greatest lessons has been that regardless of age, weight, height, or physical disability, the secret ingredient of success for those who finish a marathon (less than 1% of 1% of the world's population) is WIN*ology* Step 6: Tenacious Endurance. No matter what happens and no matter how much it hurts, you don't give up!

It's the same with any great life achievement.

Dr. Joseph Stowell, president of Cornerstone University and author of over 20 books, made a brilliant statement in his book, *Fan the Flame*.[1] He said:

No matter what happens and no matter how much it hurts, you don't give up!

"The Greeks had a race in their Olympic games that was unique. The winner was not the runner who finished first. It was the runner who finished with his torch still lit. I want to run all the way with the flame of my torch still lit."

STEP 6: TENACIOUS ENDURANCE

If you're going to win at the highest level in life, this must be your mantra:

"I'm a winner and winners never quit."

Now, on to your WIN*ology* Step 6 Assignments:

STEP 6
- TENACIOUS ENDURANCE -
ASSIGNMENTS

- Take a completely honest survey of your life. Are you more naturally prone to quit or to press through and endure, no matter what? Dig into the root behind your answer. What experiences in your life have either developed or failed to develop Tenacious Endurance in you? Express your story in your WIN*ology* journal.

- Record areas in your life in which circumstances or obstacles made (or make) you feel like throwing in the towel. Create an action plan to circumnavigate the problem and steer your path to finishing in world-class winning fashion.

WINOLOGY

- Share your findings with a couple of friends or trusted colleagues. Ask them for an outside point of view. Record your options and write out your plan.

- Build a success team. Who are the four or five people in your life that you can share your big dreams and goals with? Send them a message right now and ask to meet them for lunch or coffee within the next week. Share your personal goals and ask for their feedback and wisdom.

So, here you are at the end of Step 6, and guess what? You haven't quit! Of course you haven't. You're a WIN*ologist*. You never quit. You're a finisher. You are well on your way to winning in every area of life. There are only three more winning qualities left to discover in your WIN*ology* education. This is the phase where you see how world-class winning is exceedingly larger than you are.

WIN*OLOGY* 101

STEP 1
URGENT EXCELLENCE

STEP 2
POSITIVE CONVICTION

STEP 3
DECISIVE ACTION

STEP 4
MASTER YOUR CRAFT

STEP 5
PLAYING INBOUNDS

STEP 6
TENACIOUS ENDURANCE

9

STEP 7:
STRATEGIC PARTNERSHIP

Before entering into the world of martial arts, I loved another sport: soccer. Growing up in the 80's, soccer wasn't nearly as popular in the U.S. as it is now, so only the "chosen few" played the game. (Well, that's what I wanted to believe, anyway!) I loved every part of the game except for one—the position I played.

Playing goalie has a lot of advantages—the primary two being that you don't have to run all over the field and you can use your hands—but, it also carries some serious repercussions. Every time we lost, it seemed like I always got the blame. Usually, the team looked at me as if to say, "Well, if you had just blocked that one shot, we would've won." Of course, it felt like no one ever looked at the other 10 players who just "might've" dropped the ball during the same game. After seven years of soccer, I had my fill of shouldering the blame for every loss. Fortunately, this was about the same time my mom asked me the million-dollar question: "Hey, Joel, what do you think about trying martial arts this summer?"

Being temporarily fed up with my so-called "team" sport, I gravitated toward martial arts, mainly because it was originally an individual sport and conquest. If I won in this arena, it was due to the fact that I kicked tail and took names. If I lost, it was because I didn't handle business. My "team" only had one person, thus only one person to blame or congratulate—me.

Or so I thought.

During the first 10 years of my training and competition career, I fell into a winner's greatest deception—that I was a one-man show. I was dead wrong. Then, I came face-to-face with this stark revelation: I had *never* won any medal, championship, or title on my own. There was a team around me the entire time.

For starters, my parents constantly supported me on so many levels. They financed my training and competitions, transported me to and from the gym and events, and offered enormous emotional support throughout my entire career. Then there were my instructors—men who gave me their very best with the selfless goal of making me better than themselves. And, of course, all of my classmates and training partners who endured the blood, sweat, and tears right alongside me as we sharpened ourselves for greatness. If not for all these and an army of others, I never would have stood on any championship pedestal.

This is something every WINologist needs to know:

There's no such thing as a self-made man or woman.

Step 7: Strategic Partnership

No one grows into their success by their own merits and efforts. Show me a winner and I'll show you a team of people who contributed to his/her success. Every great success story—no matter how looming or iconic the personality may be—is a compilation of teamwork, compromise, and cooperation.

Welcome to WIN*ology* Step 7: Strategic Partnership.

- Relation-Ship -

Strategic Partnership can basically be boiled down to one word: relationships. It's the people you connect with and those who join themselves to you. It's practically impossible for me to overemphasize how important Strategic Partnership is in your journey of world-class performance. The value of connecting with the right people, at the right place, at the right time is immeasurable for your success. Rabbi Daniel Lapin says it best:

*"Your **network** equals your **net worth**."*

To become a world-class winner, you must quickly learn two things:

1. Recognize that relationships are currency.
2. See the value hidden within people who come across your path.

Notice the punctuation of this section, "Relation-ship."

No, it's not a typo, but rather a way to view those who are sent to help you accomplish your mission. Allow me to explain.

Our world is ruled by those who can maximize and monetize the shipping industry. Just look at global magnate, Jeff Bezos, for example. In 1994, he established his Internet company, Amazon.com. Bezos perceived the window of opportunity in the space of e-commerce and applied Urgent Excellence. As of March 2015, Forbes magazine reported Bezos' net worth at $34.8 billion, ranking him as the 15th wealthiest individual in the world. One of Amazon's main components to their success is shipping. Without it, products stay in warehouses and never reach the marketplace.

Amazon isn't alone. Every product has to be shipped—be it airship, landship, sea ship—to reach its maximum potential of customers. While the Industrial Revolution changed our world forever by introducing various new ways of transportation (planes, trains, ships, etc.), the original and greatest vehicle of value existed long before any of these modern-day marvels.

It's called relation-ship.

We've all heard the saying, "It's not what you know but who you know that counts." Even though I don't like downplaying the "what you know" part—and you had better have your stuff together when your time comes—the "who you know that counts" piece is very true. I like to say it like this:

Step 7: Strategic Partnership

Who you know can launch what you know to a championship level.

Do you desire to win at the highest level in your field? Then lodge this powerful truth in your brain: Your future success is riding on the strategic relationships you value, establish, *and* maintain. Establishing relationships is one thing, but it's a whole different ballgame to sustain them throughout the years.

There's never been a time in history where relationships have been more disposable. Our modern-day society has trained us to cast away those who seemingly complicate, constrain, or potentially hold us back. Today, the flippancy by which we discard relationships runs the gamut from unfriending someone on Facebook to ending multi-year marriages and business relationships—many times over petty compounding disagreements, selfishness, and differences of opinions. For some reason, "Until death do us part," or "We're in this business together all the way to the end," has been replaced by Ricky Bobby's famous words (from the movie *Talladega Nights*), "If you ain't first, you're last!"

Your future success is riding on the strategic relationships you value, establish, *and* maintain.

Whenever you have the temptation to walk away from someone who's been placed in your life to help you rise to the top, stop and ask yourself, "Is this really the right thing to do?" It could be that this "pain in the rear" might be one of your most valuable resources. Maybe it's time to reconsider. Maybe it's time to see the positive aspects they bring to your life and future, and then weigh the balance before pulling the plug. The ancient Jewish adage, "As iron sharpens iron,"[1] speaks to this reality. The people in our lives are necessary to sharpen us . . . and sharpening is rarely pleasant.

I can attest that I would never be what or who I am today without the myriad of friends, family, instructors, teachers, and pastors who prodded me on, told me the truth, and encouraged me along the way. Did I like all of them all of the time? Most certainly not! Were there disagreements and differences of opinion during the course of those relationships? Absolutely. Did I just throw people who I didn't agree with out the window of my life, anticipating the next person to jump in and take their place? No, even though I was tempted to at times! In the end, we stuck it out—even when the relation-*ship* didn't seem to be delivering the goods.

I shudder to think where I'd be today without those who sacrificed and gave of themselves for me all along my journey. Many times they saw something in me that I didn't even see in myself. I'm living proof that when you're connected to the *right* people, for the *right* reason, you position yourself to be a recipient of the *right* things— even during the times you don't deserve it!

So, how do you maintain and nurture such life-producing relationships, even with disagreements and

STEP 7: STRATEGIC PARTNERSHIP

differences?

It comes down to one word: honor.

- LIVE BY THE CODE -

With my undying passion for the martial arts, I'll give you one guess to name my all-time favorite movie growing up? (Hint: It was in the 80's.) Give up? You better believe that *The Karate Kid* was at the top of my list! (*Top Gun* and *Tombstone* were a close second and third.) I watched that movie so many times that I knew every line, not to mention every move Mr. Miagi taught his protégé, Daniel-San. More than the "crane technique" and great one-liners, the movie also taught me a very important life principle, one that's a vital ingredient in the quest for greatness: the power of honor.

To maintain Strategic Partnerships and win in life, you must adhere to an honor code. While the very mention of this term may conjure flashbacks of a code of conduct you signed at a school, civic institution, or corporation, allow me the opportunity to reshape your thinking.

When you stop and think about it, most codes of honor are a dichotomy. They contain a built-in sense of fear, as well as a potential sense of self-assurance. In the end, it comes down to this: Adhere to the code and you're "in like Flynn." Breach the code, and you're out on your ear. This, my friend, is not the type of honor required to maintain healthy Strategic Partnerships.

Honor is more than just treating someone with dignity;

it's a universal power with a gravitational pull of both good things and good people toward your life. The power of honor, as difficult as it might be to comprehend, can yield some of the greatest results in developing Strategic Partnerships and exponentially enhance your future. The keys to activate this amazing power are simple:

- Learn what honor is.
- Learn how to wield it.

Let's look at both aspects.

- Honor vs. Respect -

All throughout my martial arts training, I was forced to become well versed in the subject of honor. It was a huge part of my training. In some respect, I was Daniel-San, but instead of "paint the fence" and "sand the floor," I washed the windows and vacuumed the carpet at my instructor's command. For years, that was my life. But, just like young Daniel, I was learning a far deeper lesson than met my eye.

One of the fundamental martial arts training requirements is to treat those who are your seniors in a certain manner. This was fairly easy for me in the beginning, seeing that all of my instructors could mop the floor with me. But as I advanced in skill and rank, it became more difficult to swallow. No matter how good I became at my craft, I was still required to treat my seniors in a certain

STEP 7: STRATEGIC PARTNERSHIP

way, regardless of their proficiency or conduct. That is when I learned the real distinction between honor and respect. Simply put, respect is *conditional*; honor is *positional*.

> *. . . Respect is conditional; honor is positional.*

Respect is based on conduct and behavior, therefore it doesn't happen automatically. The old adage still rings true today: "You gain respect the old-fashioned way—you earn it!" Everybody yearns for some R.E.S.P.E.C.T. (Thank you, Aretha!), but not everyone does what's necessary to earn it. One condition that controls respect is your own core values. If someone has a track record of performing or behaving in a way that coincides with what you deem important and valuable, then respect follows. The opposite is also true.

Honor, on the other hand, isn't rooted in conduct and behavior, but rather position and title. There have been many people throughout my life that I didn't necessarily respect, but treated with honor due to their position. Quite honestly, this hasn't always been easy, but it's been one of the most valuable, positively powerful lessons of my life.

A number of years ago, I found myself working with a supervisor who was . . . Well, let's just say, he was quite difficult. Actually, demanding, rude, degrading, volatile, and manipulative would better describe him. (I think he could've been a regular on *Days of Our Lives*!) Needless to say, this individual pushed me to my limits numerous times. If I had a dollar for every time I envisioned unleashing a flurry of deadly ninja moves on him, I would have a whole lot of stinkin' money in the bank! Somehow, I mustered the ability to honor his position and keep my mouth shut—for the most part.

The results?

Unbeknownst to my supervisor, his behavior was being monitored by our CEO and board of directors. Within 18 months, he was released from his position. But, that's just half of the story.

During that same time, my behavior was also in full view. At the end of the day, the honor I bestowed upon this man—because of his position—was returned to me, with interest, by the bigwigs of the company. After my supervisor's termination, I was promoted and well-compensated. Looking back, the 18 months of suffering was well worth it. I lived by the code—the honor code—and learned a valuable lesson along the way:

Honor is a universal force.

- BACK TO YOU -

Much like the law of gravity, honor has incredible reciprocal power. The law of gravity says, "What goes up must come down." In the same way, honor has an incredibly symbiotic empowering quality. When you give honor, honor returns to you. No matter what you call it—The Golden Rule, karma, the law of sowing and reaping, or basic common sense—investing honor absolutely works.

STEP 7: STRATEGIC PARTNERSHIP

Oftentimes, honor is returned to you from the individual to whom you gave it; however, this isn't always the case. As with me and my supervisor, the honor I invested in him (even though I didn't respect him) was witnessed by others, who in turn moved to invest honor in me. The secret is to freely give honor with no strings attached. When you make the decision to honor someone, whether you respect them or not, you're not only investing into their lives, you're also investing into your own future.

Every financial investor knows the acronym ROI (return on investment). It's basically what you can expect in return for your contribution. ROI isn't limited to financial terminology; it spans every area of life. For example, if you plant apple seeds, your ROI is apples. Plant potatoes, the ROI is in potatoes, and so on. It's the same way with honor. If you invest in honor, you will receive honor in return.

This principal has proven true, time and again, with my sweet wife, Jennifer. From time to time, her sweetness is eclipsed by ... Well, let's call it ... semi-sweetness. The same is true of me. In our early years, we weren't sensitive enough to allow the power of honor to temper our responses during conversations. However, we were astonished to learn how quickly we both responded to just a dash of honor. Over the years, we've grown to understand that the honor we invest towards each other, especially in challenging times when it seems undeserved, actually pays the greatest dividends. My honor triggers a response—her honor—and vice versa.

Honor doesn't come cheap. As a matter of fact, it's an

investment of your time, energy, and even your resources. However, the relationships in your life which require this investment—your spouse, boss, parents, professors, business partners, mentors, etc.—usually have a significant potential return for your future and your quality of life. Investing into these (and other) relationships can return enormous amounts of joy and satisfaction. Take them for granted, and they will cost you dearly.

Recognizing the value and potential ROI of honor will position you to not only win in life but to remain on top. With all diligence, learn the secret of the honor code.

Invest heavily in important relationships which hold the power to significantly impact your future.

When you sow honor, you reap a life of success and winning.

Now, you might be asking, "So, how does this mysterious, intangible honor thing work?" Honestly, I'm not quite sure. It just does. I've lived it my entire life. I don't fully understand the law of gravity either, but that doesn't make me any less careful while climbing on ladders. I'm not well versed on the laws of thrust and lift, but every time I'm on an airplane, I'm glad they work!

Honor is the exact same way. It just works.

Step 7: Strategic Partnership

- Don't Kill the Magic -

As previously stated, no one becomes great on their own. The tendency, however, is that when we embrace the new, true, positive realities about ourselves, we neglect to apply the same mentality to the valuable people all around us. The ability to harness and preserve those positive realities, concerning the valuable people in our lives, is crucial in maintaining long-term relationships. It's those relationships which maximize the synergistic power of Strategic Partnership. How do you keep them?

By being grateful.

If we ever allow the deception of ungratefulness to enter our lives, our perception has the tendency to change. The "magic" begins to fade, and we stop valuing the greatness in the partners we've been given. We begin to see ourselves as much better than we should, and we view others around us as much less than they are. It doesn't take long until a lack of gratefulness towards the gift in others starts to severely limit our ability to coexist and procreate greatness. It seems world-renowned playwright, George Bernard Shaw, was on to something when he said:

> *"The most tragic thing in the world is a man of genius who is not a man of honor."*

Think about it. There's no Ricky without Lucy, no Sherlock Holmes without Dr. Watson, no Penn without Teller, no Rob without Big, and no Siegfried without Roy. Magical partnerships are magical due to the chemistry between great performers. It takes a cast of many, not just a single talent, to produce a great show. Honor is the glue that holds them together.

Roy Horn of the magical duo, Siegfried and Roy, understood honor to the degree that even after being mauled by a 400-pound tiger, he never blamed his partner, staff, or anyone else for the horrific incident. Why? Because honor doesn't point fingers; honor invests in the future. What's even more incredible is that Roy even honored and protected the white tiger, Manticore—a vital part of the cast and a valuable contributor to the duo's great success—who maimed him and left him paralyzed.

What some would call crazy, WIN*ology* calls dedication and commitment to the magic. Even with legendary solo acts, such as The Great Houdini or David Copperfield, their greatness was only as great as their supporting staff. The magicians' captivating illusions lay at the mercy of beautiful assistants, stage hands, grips, and technicians—all who made the magic come alive.

Honor in relationships is what keeps the magic happening.

- Do What it Takes -

Investing in strategic relationships is exactly that: an investment. Showing honor and gratefulness to those who are placed in your life to help you succeed is an investment of your time, energy, and even money. Take action to show your gratefulness. Send a card, give a gift, make a phone call, set up lunches (and *you* pay for them),

Step 7: Strategic Partnership

etc. Communicate your thankfulness for that person being in your life on a regular basis. Always remember these three powerful points about honor:

- *Honoring* your Strategic Partnerships guides and protects your future.
- *Losing* those partnerships will cost you more than you can ever imagine.
- *Investing* in those relationships will bring more ROI than you ever expected.

So, let's move on to your WIN*ology* Step 7: Strategic Partnership Assignments.

STEP 7
- Strategic Partnership -
Assignments

- Make a list of your strategic relationships. Beside each one, write how they are/have been instrumental in contributing to your greatness and success.

- For each of those people, make a list of their great qualities.

- Write out specific ideas and ways you can intentionally honor each individual in the most meaningful way.

- Commit to invest in those strategic relationships. Be thoughtful and specific and, most importantly, follow through.

Strategic Partnership is a major element to winning and *staying* a winner. Honor and gratefulness are the keys which keep them connected to you. I challenge you to let one of your life's mottos reflect the powerful, timeless words of William Shakespeare:

> *"If it be a sin to covet honor, I am the most offending soul."*

Fortunately, you need not covet hopelessly. You have the secret: Follow the honor code. Your future is bright. Strategic Partnership holds the key.

WIN*OLOGY* 101

STEP 1
URGENT EXCELLENCE

STEP 2
POSITIVE CONVICTION

STEP 3
DECISIVE ACTION

STEP 4
MASTER YOUR CRAFT

STEP 5
PLAYING INBOUNDS

STEP 6
TENACIOUS ENDURANCE

STEP 7
STRATEGIC PARTNERSHIP

10

STEP 8:
CONTAGIOUS KINDNESS

New York City artist, Martin Kornfeld, was on to something when he created a noteworthy artistic piece a few years ago. In 2013, passers-by of his Greenwich Village townhome began to notice that "Marty," as friends call him, had taken it upon himself to release a little bit of sunshine into the world, starting with his own neighborhood.

Using all the colors of the rainbow, Kornfeld painted and hung a sign that read, "If we all do one random act of kindness daily, we might just set the world in the right direction." The artist's work was a tribute in memory of his mother, who insisted that her children do two random acts of kindness every day. Kornfeld took it another step further, offering hand-painted posters of his quote to anyone interested.

New York City artists aren't the only ones turning their attention toward the contagious tendencies of kindness. Political scientist, James Fowler, of the University of

California, San Diego and medical sociologist, Nicholas Christikas, of Harvard University have taken notice, as well. On March 8, 2010, the Proceedings of the National Academy of Sciences published Fowler and Christikas's extraordinary experimental findings.[1]

In a series of tests, participants played a game where each one was allotted a certain sum of money. Their instructions were easy: (1.) Keep as much money as they desired and (2.) Donate as much as they desired to a common pot shared by the other players. This wasn't a team game; all were seeking their own individual benefit. The findings of the game were extremely interesting and conclusive.

From round to round, the more certain anonymous players made large contributions to the community pot, the more generous and kind the entire playing field became. The conclusion? Open acts of kindness and generosity provoke others to do the same.

But artists and researchers aren't alone. Others have documented this exact phenomenon.

In her 2010 *Helix Magazine* article, journalist Shannon Mehner records:

> *"Kindness is contagious, according to a study done by researchers at University of California, Los Angeles and University of Cambridge and University of Plymouth in the United Kingdom. When we see someone else help another person it gives us a good feeling, which in turn causes us to go out and do*

Step 8: Contagious Kindness

something altruistic ourselves the study found; which was the first of its kind to systematically document this tendency in human nature."[2]

Cambridge's Simone Schnall led a 2009 research study, conducted by the U.S. Bureau of Labor and Statistics, which found that 1.6 million more people volunteered in 2009 than in 2008.[3] This raises the question: Why are people being so nice? Schnall's response was, "When you feel this sense of moral 'elevation,' not only do you say you want to be a better person and help others, but you actually do when the opportunity presents itself."

Schnall's use of the term, "elevation," was actually coined by one of our founding fathers, Thomas Jefferson. Jefferson's term, "elevation," is defined as *a specific human sense far greater than mere happiness*. Elevation is the emotion we experience when we see someone else engaged in acts of kindness.

Scientific research, behavioral studies, and modern art have all found WIN*ology*'s Step 8 to be true: Kindness is contagious.

- Sometimes, Son . . . -

In our dog-eat-dog world, kindness is rarely seen as an attribute of winners. "Good guys finish last" has been heralded for years, mainly from those trying to excuse themselves from basic human courtesies. But these mindsets could not be further from the truth. Instead of good guys finishing last, my observations have been, "Bad guys finish alone."

Think about it. What does it matter if you finish on top in your vocation, exploits, and finances, if you lose your most precious commodities along the way? Things like your spouse, children, friends, strategic partners, etc. Such is the story of far too many wealthy, so-called "successful" people. Winning the wrong way will cause you to end up alone and empty despite all your accomplishments. But, it doesn't have to be that way.

You can win *and* be contagiously kind along the way.

My father, Ken, has lived an exemplary illustration of Contagious Kindness in front of me my entire life. The consummate gentleman, my father has always been the one who opens doors for others, helps grandmas cross the street, and does whatever he can to better the lives of those around him. Simply put, Pops never met a stranger.

I'll never forget the day I came home to find my dad mowing a single mother's yard across the street from our house. Now, in the suburb of Tulsa, OK where I grew up, yards were formidable to say the least. These lush fields of St. Augustine weren't postage stamp-sized, as is so prevalent in today's suburban neighborhoods. No, these were real yards... with real, thick grass.

As a young teenager who would do just about anything to relieve myself of manual labor, I was astounded to see my dad pushing that mower through thick, overgrown, 12-inch-tall grass... in someone else's yard, nonetheless. I asked him, "Pops, what are you doing? Why are you

Step 8: Contagious Kindness

mowing Ms. Robyn's yard? Is she paying you to do that?" His response was baffling.

"No, Joel. She's not paying me. Robyn is all alone and doesn't have anyone to help her. Sometimes, son, you do things just because it's the right thing to do." He had no idea how much those words would shape the philosophy of my life. In that moment, Pop's selfless, Contagious Kindness provoked me to action.

- Courteous and Calculating -

There was a day and age when kindness and courtesy ruled. It was a time when people were concerned about the needs of their fellow man and intentionally sought to enhance the lives of others. It's time to go retro. It's time to reclaim the lost art of kindness.

Today, the overwhelming fear of "ladder climbers" is this: "If I'm nice and kind, someone will take advantage of me." What they fail to realize is the difference between kindness and naiveté. Being kind doesn't mean you become ignorant to the evil some people possess. You can be kind and yet not position yourself to become a victim of bad people. It's possible to be *courteous* and *calculating* at the same time.

This type of Contagious Kindness is what the first Christians were taught by their Messiah back in the first century: to be gentle as doves, yet simultaneously shrewd as serpents.[4] In fact, regardless of your religion or lack thereof, you'll need to learn this ancient art of cunning, yet sincere, kindness to sustain a life of winning. The secret to sustainable victory in life is helping others win along the way.

> **The secret to sustainable victory in life is helping others win along the way.**

Obviously, there are certain competitions and areas of life where there's only one winner; however, other areas may host multiple victors. Just as the universal law of honor contains the power to sustain your winning position, the principle of Contagious Kindness melds perfectly with honor, taking the enlightenment of investing into the realm of humanity one step further. Every WIN*ologist* must come to this understanding:

While you're reaching upward for the stars in your quest to become world-class in your field, never forget to reach back and pull others up with you.

Helping others win promotes health and loyalty. It also insures that when you attain your goals and are ready to celebrate your accomplishments, people will actually come to your party! Without Contagious Kindness, victories are simply less satisfying and ultimately less sustainable.

Step 8: Contagious Kindness

- Band of Brothers -

The great Ralph Waldo Emerson is noted for saying: "The only way to have a friend is to be one." Here's my addition to this quote, which you might find contradictive at first:

> ***Your competitors may also wind up being your friends.***

While competing on the world stage in martial arts, some of my greatest friends were also my fiercest rivals. As strange as it may seem, we shared a very real comradery along with a common goal: We all wanted to win. But we also trained together to sharpen each other's skills. As we prepared for competitions, we actually enhanced each other's abilities; and we all improved along the way. We were a band of competing brothers, connected by our ancient art and quest for victory.

On tournament days, it was a different dynamic. If we were fighting against each other, we would jokingly say, "I'll see you in two minutes," while touching gloves. Once the bell rang and the gloves touched, it was on!

Before and after the match, we were the closest of friends. During the match, we were fierce competitors. Oddly enough, this balance forged us into the most finely-tuned competitors we could be. And, here's what we discovered: Winning is simply more fun when you win with somebody else.

You can experience a win-win.

- WIN-WIN -

I have a very dear friend—and strategic partner—named James Mathews. James and I have been uniquely connected our entire lives. We first met in 1996 at a small community meeting for young married couples. Over the next few years, we found ourselves reconnecting and reuniting at various and unrelated locations. You can only imagine our enthusiasm when we discovered that our parents had been friends since back in the 1970's. Needless to say, there's a touch of destiny in our relationship.

Known as the Indian "Dos Equis Man," James is often referred to by many of his friends as "the most interesting man in the world." (Although, he prefers the pseudonym "The Indian Forrest Gump," since somehow he's done almost everything imaginable.) With his connections to the White House, the Rockefeller Foundation, Mumbai's Bollywood, and even the Indian Prime Minister's office, James is truly a fascinating man. I'm also proud to say that he has embodied the principles of WIN*ology* for decades!

One night a number of years ago, James taught me a very valuable lesson while we were discussing one of the most vital parts of doing business—negotiation. During our conversation (in which I did most of the listening), James enlightened me on some of his negotiation tactics he employed while "doing deals" on the highest level of international business. I was amazed and shocked at his approach.

James said, "I always let the other side win first." "What?" I exclaimed. "Can you explain exactly how that

STEP 8: CONTAGIOUS KINDNESS

works?" He said, "Joel, I'm going for a win. I know I'm going to win, but my secret is to always let whomever I'm negotiating with win first. As long as they feel like they're winning, they're completely happy with me achieving my desired outcome, as well."

Needless to say, I was incredibly intrigued.

James' ultra-successful negotiation technique boils down to this: He has mastered the art of Contagious Kindness; so much so, that the people he was negotiating with felt so good about their position, they gladly gave him everything he wanted in return. It truly was a "win-win" deal!

The truth is, you don't have to be negotiating multi-million-dollar business deals to experience the joy of a win-win. You can enjoy those scenarios with the people around you, right now. This brown-nosing, dog-eat-dog, survival-of-the-fittest mumbo jumbo we've been sold on for so many years is a total lie. Yes, you can adhere to it and seemingly win . . . for a while, but in the end you'll likely find yourself alone and dissatisfied. The antidote for this nonsense is quite simple: Helping others win is one of the greatest ways of ensuring victory yourself.

And kindness is the key.

> **Helping others win is one of the greatest ways of ensuring victory yourself.**

- Pay it Forward -

In the 2007 blockbuster movie, *Evan Almighty*, Congressman Evan Baxter (played brilliantly by multiple award-winning actor, Steve Carell) has a visitation from "God" and becomes a modern-day Noah.[5] After building this ark and saving his city from impending danger, Evan has a conversation with "God" (played by the epic Morgan Freeman). In this dialog, God explains the importance of the modern-day ark:

> *God:* "How do we change the world?"
>
> *Evan:* "One act of random kindness at a time."
>
> *God:* "One **A**ct of **R**andom **K**indness at a time— ARK."

More than just a great movie scene, "God" and Evan unveiled a powerful truth. It's true, random acts of kindness *can* change the world, creating a positive ripple effect and restoring our faith in love and compassion of the human spirit.

Many years ago, I worked with a team to organize a life-enriching experience for 40 students. For one week, these teenagers would leave all the comforts of their North Dallas suburbanite lifestyles and serve as social workers in some of the roughest areas surrounding south central Los Angeles. These seven days would allow them the opportunity to impact people far less fortunate than themselves. But, in the end, their lives—along with mine—would be the most changed.

STEP 8: CONTAGIOUS KINDNESS

On the last night of our trip, my friend, Mike, and I were crossing the street at the corner of Ivars and Hollywood Boulevard. We were making a run for some frozen yogurt, when we happened upon a very interesting man, Victor Estrada. Though his last name was recognizably attached to my favorite late 1970's Hollywood actor, Erik Estrada of *CHIPS*, Victor was anything but a famed Hollywood actor. Conversely, he was a homeless criminal, on the run and addicted to drugs. Our innocent yogurt run was about to get really interesting.

At first glance, we would have never known Victor's current state, seeing that he was dressed relatively sharp. (We later learned he had stolen the clothes earlier that day.) After our initial, "How do you do?" Victor was quick to offer his quest to purchase drugs. Obviously, an interesting conversation ensued, which ended with us praying for Victor and offering to find him help. But prayer was just the beginning.

The opportunity to spread kindness was staring us right in the face—and we responded.

When we found out the clothes Victor had stolen were his only wardrobe, Mike quickly took off his hoodie sweatshirt and handed it to him. Then, we took him to the mission center where we were staying and Victor had his fill of hamburgers. (He actually took some with him!) Lastly, and most importantly, Mike gave him his own Bible.

With a belly full of hamburgers, a new sweatshirt, and a Bible, Victor's countenance had completely shifted so much that he was trying to give his food away to others in need. He was also encouraging everyone around him with the kindest words—behavior not expected from a homeless drug addict. Something was happening. Kindness was spreading. Understandably, skeptics would assume this was all part of his scam, mainly because his initial inquiry was to score drugs. But the ending of this story would prove them all wrong.

Our search for hotel accommodations for our newfound friend came up empty. Due to the fact he had no form of ID, no one would take him in. Once again, Victor was forced to sleep on the streets. Hoping for the best, we hugged and said our goodbyes. We couldn't help but to assume this would be the last time we'd see Vic, but we were in for a huge surprise.

The very next morning, guess who showed up at our building, still gripping his Bible in his hand? Victor! His only reason for stopping by was to show his gratitude—nothing more. He didn't ask for money. We even offered, but he declined saying that he didn't need it. After exchanging a few pleasantries, Victor told us that he was on the way to turn himself in for the crimes he had recently committed. He decided to get clean, pay for his wrongdoings, and make a fresh start! This was great news, but there was more. Victor surprised us yet again.

Before he left, I asked him, "Hey, man, where's your new hoodie sweatshirt?" Victor answered, "I gave it to a lady last night on the street. She needed it way worse than me." This, my friend, is the power of paying Contagious Kindness forward!

It's real, and it works!

STEP 8: CONTAGIOUS KINDNESS

- OPEN YOUR EYES -

Stories like this are rare, but they shouldn't be! When's the last time you went out of your way to help someone you didn't know? Or better yet, someone who couldn't help you in return? Let's take it a step further. Who are the people who seem to be your competitors, but you have the ability to sharpen and enhance? Believe me, they're all around you—probably right under your nose. The real question is: Can you recognize these opportunities for kindness? Many times we are too blinded by our own pursuits to see those positioned alongside us for great win-win opportunities. Open your eyes. Opportunities await.

Your Step 8: Contagious Kindness Assignments are next!

STEP 8
- CONTAGIOUS KINDNESS -
ASSIGNMENTS

♦ Take an honest inventory. Is kindness a natural reflex to you or do you have to work at it? What would your strategic partners say? Ask them.

- Do you tend to easily trust or be a bit naïve? Or do you assume everyone has an agenda? Think about it for a moment and list how you could find a harmonious balance of shrewd kindness.

- Can you recollect any time recently when you could've been more kind or thoughtful? Maybe to a co-worker who was having a bad day and needing encouragement or even help? Maybe to a needy person on the street? Or, maybe to someone who looked lost and in need of direction, but you were too busy or consumed in your own life to take a moment? Resolve to become more aware, available, and action-minded. Be ready to walk out Contagious Kindness.

As you go through your assignments, remember these words from renowned American author, Mark Twain:

"Kindness is the language which the deaf can hear and the blind can see."

When you speak the language of kindness, you discover one of WIN*ology*'s greatest secrets:

Step 8: Contagious Kindness

Life is so much sweeter when you live to enrich others.

Now, get ready for the ninth and final step of WIN*ology* in discovering the anchoring power of your life: Great Love.

WIN*OLOGY* 101

STEP 1
URGENT EXCELLENCE

STEP 2
POSITIVE CONVICTION

STEP 3
DECISIVE ACTION

STEP 4
MASTER YOUR CRAFT

STEP 5
PLAYING INBOUNDS

STEP 6
TENACIOUS ENDURANCE

STEP 7
STRATEGIC PARTNERSHIP

STEP 8
CONTAGIOUS KINDNESS

11

STEP 9:
GREAT LOVE

Congratulations! You are a finisher. You're well on your way to becoming the very best version of "you" that you can possibly be: a true champion! Believe it or not, you're about to learn the most valuable lesson of all. But before we begin, let's briefly recap your journey up to this point.

So far, you've discovered the power of Urgent Excellence, developed a Positive Conviction, declared and taken Decisive Action, begun to Master Your Craft, learned the value of Playing Inbounds, moved forward with Tenacious Endurance through adversity, aligned yourself with and honored crucial, Strategic Partnerships, and showed Contagious Kindness. That's seriously impressive.

Now, there's only one step remaining on your WIN*ology* journey: finding your Great Love.

Before you start thinking, "Wait, I have to be in a serious relationship with someone to be a WIN*ologist*?" let me assure you of one thing: I'm not talking about finding the "love of your life" in this context. However, during the course of discovering your Great Love, you very well may find the love of your life along the way. Truly, finding and fulfilling your Great Love makes you pretty darn attractive!

Now that I have your attention...

People who find their Great Love are the ones living satisfying lives of passion and purpose. On the other hand, there are those who reach the pinnacle of success in their field but never find the secret of their personal Great Love. Although they wind up rich and successful, there's something missing. Thus, the secret of this final WIN*ology* step:

Finding your Great Love is finding your "Why."

- Two Most Important Days -

In his great book, *Start with Why*, author Simon Sinek does a fantastic job illuminating the truth on this subject.[1] His writings reveal the value of understanding the "Why" of a matter before taking action. Sinek reiterates that before you launch any vision or attempt to mobilize and inspire other leaders to rally around the cause, you first must know the "Why" of the matter. He's 100% right.

But I'm talking about an even greater "Why."

The "Why" I'm referring to lies deep within your own soul. It's hidden so deep that many fail to find it, even after achieving and transcending many levels of success. Factually, it's not uncommon for people to be in their 40's

Step 9: Great Love

or 50's and yet remain unsuccessful in identifying their Great Love, mainly because they fail to ask the right questions. While they may have "arrived," they still don't know "Why." Consequently, this is a major reason why it's so prevalent in our society for people to experience a midlife crisis.

One of my favorite all-time quotes comes from Mark Twain. He said:

> **"The two most important days of your life are the day you were born and the day you find out why."**

Even though many people go through their entire life only recognizing one of those days, this doesn't have to be the case. It is possible to discover the more important day—the "Why" day, the day that gives life eternal significance. WIN*ologists* are people who discover both days.

While it's one thing to understand the simple, smaller "Why" tied to personal or professional goals and objectives, discovering your global "Why" is an entirely different level of understanding. It's what penetrates to the very core of your being and becomes the reason behind everything you do.

If you haven't discovered your "Why" yet, don't worry. You're going to find it. I'm going to help you, because finding your Great Love is all about asking the right questions.

In the epic movie, *Gladiator*, General Maximus Aurelius declared, "What you do in life echoes in eternity." This larger-than-life character's declaration was more correct than many people realize. Every human being is searching for significance that transcends beyond their own life. But significance isn't only found in the "What." Significance is also found in the "Why."

Our "Why" fuels "What" we do.

Until you discover your Great Love—your "Why"— you risk living a life of doing the right things for the wrong reasons. Today, that all changes!

Now, you will start the journey of recognizing your second most important day—your "Why" day.

- Something's Changing -

In the fall of 1999, I was 26 years old and at the peak of my competition career. I felt like the sky was the limit. Every door I could have imagined was opening for me, and I couldn't fathom life being any better. I was the reigning world champion, had secured a seat on the Global Taekwondo Federation's U.S. team, owned multiple businesses. Even better, I was madly in love with my beautiful, young wife, Jennifer. We had everything: careers, money, significance, stuff—you name it, we had it. I was living every one of my dreams... or so I thought.

Over a period of a few months, I experienced some very strange and unusual encounters. First, I began to have dreams during the night in which I could see myself 10 years older. I was still in the same field of business I'd been in since my Taekwondo instructor hired me at 14

Step 9: Great Love

but something was remarkably different. In my dream, I was miserable! Somehow, it was showing me that I'd missed a significant window of opportunity, and now I was stuck.

Then, I began to feel and deal with strange new emotions. Part of our martial art's studio business model involved the public school system. Routinely, we were on school campuses performing exhibitions, pep rallies, and conducting drug-free assemblies for Red Ribbon Week. I had done this for years, but never once had I experienced anything like what was about to happen.

Right in the middle of one of my high school assemblies, I became overwhelmed with emotion. Up to this point, I had spoken at hundreds of school assemblies, telling my own story of dealing with peer pressure, making bad decisions, and learning life the hard way—but this time it was very different. In this assembly, I actually started to cry! That's right, you heard me. Crying . . . in public . . . in front of a bunch of high-schoolers I didn't even know! It was horrifying.

Here I was, supposedly this world champion tough guy, and I'm crying like a baby, pleading with these kids not to make the same mistakes I made at their age. And, it happened more than once. The first time, I

> . . . Significance isn't only found in the "What." Significance is also found in the "Why."

wrote it off as just being a bad day. The second time was more concerning. But the third time? I thought I was losing my mind!

How well I remember walking to my car after that third assembly, giving myself a piece of my own mind, and complaining to God all at the same time. I specifically remember muttering, "What the heck is going on? God, what are You doing to me?"

And then, it happened.

The moment that literally changed my life forever.

- The Aha Moment -

Somewhere from within the deepest parts of me, I heard these words, "Joel, you're finding your true passion. It's people, Joel. People are your passion." For the first time, the thought crossed my mind, Maybe this experience that felt so hellish was actually more connected to Heaven.

Up until this time, I was convinced of my passion: my art form and the carrying on of its centuries-old tradition. No one could have persuaded me otherwise. I thought competing—and more specifically, winning—was my passion. What I was soon to learn was that these were my little "whys," but my global "Why"—a passion for people—had been staring me square in the face the entire time.

Quite honestly, this "aha" moment took me totally by surprise, but it revolutionized my life.

What I quickly came to realize was that the martial arts,

Step 9: Great Love

the competitions, and winning were nothing more than vehicles used to connect me to my real passion: the people who were involved. But it wasn't just the people themselves that made me tick. What really ignited my fire was the ability to help, train, enhance, and elevate their lives to a new level. Then, it hit me like a ton of bricks:

My Great Love was calling me from deep within.

This initial "knowing," while awesome in its context, also carried a huge challenge. I quickly realized that I had to venture out of my vocational field. For the first time in my adult life, I was about to jump out of my place of comfort, to identify and forge a path into virgin territory. For me to live my Great Love to its fullest, I had to discover other areas which would allow me the opportunity to explore the depths of people's hearts, minds, and souls. Somewhere, there had to be a venue where I could deposit the secrets of thinking like a world-class competitor into the lives of individuals in an entirely different way.

My "aha" moment had brought me face to face with the final stage of WIN*ology*. Now I was about to reset my process and start all over in a brand new field.

I felt a sense of Urgent Excellence. An open window of opportunity was looming. I didn't know where it would come from or how I would get through it; I just knew it was there. That urgency, combined with my faith and Positive Conviction, compelled me to take Decisive Action and begin to master a brand new craft.

Within six months after my defining moment, I completely walked away from my field as a professional martial artist. I left everything. It was a terrifying leap of faith. At times I second-guessed myself, fearing we might lose everything. But, the exact opposite happened.

We gained everything.

Within a few months of my decision, I took a full-time intern position at my church, working with . . . (You guessed it.) Teenagers! I was back in school, so to speak, learning an entirely new way of employing my skill set. Actually, I was pioneering the WIN*ology* system, applying my natural experiences to conquests of the soul and spirit. This journey of shaping young hearts and minds made me feel so alive. Convincing young people that they could live legendary lives by learning to think, speak, and act in the right manner was exhilarating. Quite honestly, and much to my surprise, it was the most rewarding season of life I'd ever experienced; . . . and it was just the beginning.

Since the summer of 2000 until the present, I have dedicated myself to helping others find their way. Young or old, black or white, rich or poor, male or female, owners and leaders of major corporations or clerks and baggers at retail stores—no one is exempt from the benefits of the power of WIN*ology*. The system has worked on every single one of those who were fearless enough to finish. Thousands of individuals have learned the secrets you now have access to. The ultimate goal is the same for everyone: to find your own Great Love.

Step 9: Great Love

- Deep Calling -

Something deep within you is calling out to you. Maybe you've heard it, maybe you haven't. Maybe it's too soon, and you're in the discovery process. Regardless of where you are, I promise you, your Great Love is calling from deep within you.

I was 12 years into my career and at a very crucial moment of decision when I heard it. Even though I didn't know my global "Why" throughout this period of time, I did find it. You will, too. Your Great Love is connected to the meaning of your life—something you can absolutely find and know. But the meaning of life isn't found in asking questions and philosophizing about meaning; the meaning of life is found in the living. It's discovered as you walk out your personal journey.

No one uncovers their Great Love in the same fashion. It's different for everyone. The key is to listen and be sensitive to the voice calling out within you. Don't dismiss it as "coincidence" or "happenstance." It's very real and already inside you. If you continue to listen, you *will* hear it. Here's something that will help you recognize that voice: Your deep calling is greater than you.

Operating and living in the WIN*ology* system—thinking, speaking, and acting like the true world-class winner you were born to be—will give you more opportunities to connect to a cause greater than yourself. Finding such a cause not only engages your heart and soul, but also fuels your passion for life.

Coming to the realization that your life and success

are a part of something much larger than you changes your outlook. It's one thing to grab this concept intellectually, but when you actually begin to live it out physically, your whole life changes. You finally find your reason for perpetuating this cycle of winning and transcend into a benevolent benefactor. You become a change agent in the world and in the lives around you. No longer are you winning for you; you're winning for countless others who will benefit in the wake of your success.

> No longer are you winning for you; you're winning for countless others who will benefit in the wake of your success.

Does this sound too far-fetched? I don't think so. Scores of people have already lived this type of life. Let's take a look at a few people who found their Great Love, connected to causes greater than themselves, and exist to enhance the world around them.

- Billions of Reasons -

In June of 2010, Warren Buffet, along with Bill and Melinda Gates, conspired together to create a fraternal organization of billionaires. The mission of this organization wasn't so everyone could lounge on each other's 600-foot yachts or globetrot on G5 intercontinental jets; the mission was completely opposite. The organization,

Step 9: Great Love

aptly named The Giving Pledge, called for billionaires to put their money where their mouth was. How were they to accomplish such a feat? By pledging to give away a minimum of 50% of their wealth within their lifetimes! The results? It took off like a rocket.

To date, 137 billionaires and their families from 14 countries have joined The Giving Pledge, vowing to use their amassed wealth to make the world a better place. Billionaire individuals like the founders of Facebook, AOL, eBay, Spanx, and Chobani have all pledged extreme generosity and, at the same time, declared their Great Love.

These world industry leaders have given us billions of reasons to sit up and take notice. Obviously, they know something we don't know; they see something we can't see and have experienced something we have yet to experience. What is it? In all their efforts to acquire great wealth, these elite men and women have found one of the true secrets to success: It actually *is* more blessed to give than to receive.

The Giving Pledge movement is one of the strongest testimonies of this final step of WIN*ology*. An entire organization of billionaires who have absolutely everything, yet realizing that without connecting to their own Great Love, they will never be satisfied. These men and women are the greatest collaborative group of philanthropists the world has ever known. A figurative school of whales, they are living for something larger than themselves and are making huge waves felt all around the globe.

Not only has The Giving Pledge given us a billion

reasons to notice the advantage of this giving lifestyle, there are also a billion reasons that will try to convince you otherwise. You have to make the conscious decision to rise above each one of them.

- WHY WAIT? -

While the thought of billionaires connecting to and making a significant investment in their Great Love is motivating, the beauty lies in this truth: You don't have to wait until you've "arrived" to find this true sense of meaning and purpose. In fact, most people who say, "I'll be generous when I'm rich," tend to never arrive at that moment. Why? Because the target called "rich" keeps moving, allowing excuses to arise and convince us to renegotiate.

Many years ago, Jennifer and I decided to live our lives in such a way that we always give back. We're not alone. In fact, thousands of upwardly-mobile people over the years have encircled us and taken this same pledge. These aren't billionaires; some are barely thousand-aires! They're everyday people who vowed to live a life of giving and investing in both individual lives and causes greater than themselves. They never let their economic status stop their commitment.

For Jennifer and I, we made the decision as newlyweds, way back in 1995, to give a minimum of 10% of our gross income away to the causes most valuable to our hearts: our church, and charitable organizations that make the world better. That's exactly what we did. But, it didn't

Step 9: Great Love

stop there. Over the years, we have incrementally grown our pledge as high as 15%, and our goal is to keep increasing the percentages for the remainder of our lives. Why? Because generous people are the happiest people on earth! My thought is: *Why should all the billionaires have all the fun?*

It's true, people who connect to causes bigger than themselves—giving of their time, effort, and portions of their income—are the ones who receive the biggest return on their investment along the way. Practicing generosity has brought us incredible joy for these last two decades. It may not be billions, but to us it's big, Most of all, we know we're making a big difference in the lives of those it benefits. Amazingly, even with all our giving, we have never lacked for anything.

Giving didn't leave us with less, it actually left us with more.

> **. . . Generous people are the happiest people on earth!**

- Skeptics Beware -

I know this is a hard subject for some to swallow. The idea of giving away precious hours of their time or increasing percentages of their hard-earned dollars seems ludicrous to some. I hear you. There have been times when we've even questioned if it was necessary, especially when finances were tight. It was in one of those moments I heard my mentor and pastor, Mike Hayes, say something that riveted my heart. He said, "Concerning generosity, if you can't live on 90% of your income, you probably can't live on 100% either!" This quickly made me realize that giving wasn't the issue; budgeting was the culprit.

A close friend of mine, Kevin, flipped out when he first heard me talking about this type of generosity—and he is a generous guy. His response to me was, "Ten percent huh? Are you kidding me? Dang! That's a lot of money!" To which I laughed hysterically and responded, "You're right. It *is* a lot of money, and what I receive in return is worth every dime."

I, for one, am richer for it. You can be, too.

If this step of WIN*ology* seems too challenging, pause with me for a moment and let's revisit our Step 2: Positive Conviction. The essential ingredient of this step is identifying negativity, skepticism, and doubt and replacing them with new, true positive realities. This subsequently creates corresponding new, true, positive declarations that align with your reality. From here, you begin to build your future with your words. Sound familiar? It should.

In your quest to discover your own Great Love—the global "Why" of your whole life—generosity is the key to discovery. Don't allow fear to stop you now. You've come much too far to turn back. And besides, WIN*ologists* never quit.

Finish your course and live life to the fullest, starting right now.

Step 9: Great Love

– Your Personal Mission –

Stephen Covey, author of the world-renowned, *7 Habits of Highly Effective People*, encourages those in pursuit of their cause and mission in life to write a personal mission statement for their lives.[2] He said:

> *"Writing or reviewing a mission statement changes you, because it forces you to think through your priorities deeply, carefully and to align your behavior with your beliefs."*

According to Covey, a personal mission consists of three primary parts:

- **What** do I want to **do**?
- **Who** do I want to **help**?
- **What** is the **result** and **what value** will I **create**?

Take a moment to answer these questions honestly, and begin to develop your personal mission statement. Take out your WIN*ology* journal and write down these questions:

- What people group or cause fires me up?
- When do I feel most passionate about life?
- What area or organization do I feel like I can really make a difference in?

Now, take a moment and write down your responses. This is the beginning of your personal mission statement, your first step in discovering your Great Love.

- THE NEW YOU! -

Here's a good litmus test in finding your Great Love: Any cause you're not willing to invest your time and money in is not your cause. Why? It's simple.

Love gives, and Great Love gives greatly.

It's impossible to love something or someone and not give in response to that love. When people fall in love, they spare no expense to win the other's affection. When you deeply love your children, you will do whatever it takes to create opportunities to see them happy. Being willing to significantly give towards a cause (not just a token of your appreciation) is an internal signal of your true love for what it represents. Your monetary investment in any area speaks volumes about what is truly important to you. The ancient proverb is right, "Where your treasure is, there your heart is also."[3]

Now, let's wrap up this chapter and complete our study in The Science of Winning by going a step deeper. Your Great Love Assignments for Step 9 are next!

STEP 9: GREAT LOVE

STEP 9
- GREAT LOVE -
ASSIGNMENTS

- How many hours per month can you dedicate toward a cause that moves you?
- What percentage of your income are you willing to dedicate toward your causes?
- Make the changes to your schedule and budget. Sacrifice if need be. Make a commitment and stay with it.

Take all the time you need to walk out these final steps. Then anticipate the long-term rewards of your generosity. I can promise you, you will never regret connecting with your Great Love and living your life accordingly.

- CONGRATULATIONS! -

You did it! You've completed your initial course in WIN*ology*! Now, you're in an elite class of winners with a massive future ahead of you. As you continue your climb to the top, revisit these steps and refresh yourself in the concepts and principles. Remember, they are chronological steps designed to build upon each other. From time to time you may find yourself stuck in a previous cycle due to life changes or setbacks. Don't worry; it's perfectly normal. Drop back to the previous step, review, and then continue on to greatness.

These are principles and truths I have studied for decades and will continue to do so for the rest of my life. Albert Einstein said, "Once you stop learning, you start dying!" I don't know about you, but I think it's too early to start dying! There's always more to learn and achieve, always a greater season to move towards.

Remember the words of Winston Churchill: "Never, never, never, never give up." You are a warrior and a world-class winner. The way of a winner is a life full of constant, never-ending improvement. You, my friend, are becoming a modern-day warrior poet. You are a world-class winner. The world is your canvas. Express yourself and find your own Great Love.

Here's to your ultimate success!

WIN*OLOGY* 101

STEP 1
URGENT EXCELLENCE

STEP 2
POSITIVE CONVICTION

STEP 3
DECISIVE ACTION

STEP 4
MASTER YOUR CRAFT

STEP 5
PLAYING INBOUNDS

STEP 6
TENACIOUS ENDURANCE

STEP 7
STRATEGIC PARTNERSHIP

STEP 8
CONTAGIOUS KINDNESS

STEP 9
GREAT LOVE

Endnotes

2 - The Science of Winning
1. *Oxford Dictionary of English*, Oxford University Press, 2010, eISBN: 9780191727665.
2. "Uptown Funk." Words by Mark Ronson, featuring Bruno Mars. RCA Records, 2014.

3 - Step 1: Urgent Excellence
1. *8 Mile.* Film written by Scott Silver; directed by Curtis Hanson, starring Eminem. Universal Pictures, 2002.
2. "Lose Yourself." Written, produced, and performed by Eminem. Soundtrack of the American biographical film, *8 Mile*.

4 - Step 2: Positive Conviction
1. Proverbs 23:7.
2. Leaf, Dr. Caroline. *Who Switched Off My Brain.*
3. Proverbs 23:7.
4. Ibid.

6 - Step 4: Master Your Craft
1. Collins, Jim. *Good to Great: Why Some Companies Make the Leap...and Others Don't.* HarperBusiness, 2001.
2. *Whiplash.* Film written and directed by Damien Chazelle. Bold Films, Blumhouse Productions, and Right of Way Films., 2014.

8 - Step 6: Tenacious Endurance
1. Stowell, Dr. James. *Fan the Flame: Living Out Your First Love for Christ.* Moody Press, 1986.

9 - Step 7: Strategic Partnership
1. Proverbs 27:17.

10 - Step 8: Contagious Kindness
1. https://helix.northwestern.edu/article/kindness-contagious-new-study-finds.

2. Ibid.
3. http://www.wired.com/2010/03/kindness-spreads/.
3. Matthew 10:16.
4. *Evan Almighty*. Film written by Steve Oedekerk (Screenplay), Joel Cohen, and Alec Sokolow; directed by Tom Shadyac, starring Steve Carell and Morgan Freeman. NBC Universal, 2007.

11 - STEP 9: GREAT LOVE

1. Senek, Simon. *Start with Why: How Great Leaders Inspire Everyone to Action.* Portfolio, 2009
2. Covey, Stephen. *7 Habits of HIghly Effective People.* Simon Schuster Ltd. UK; Illustrated. Edition, 1990.
3. Matthew 6:21.

– About the Author –
Joel Scrivner

Joel Scrivner is a former six-time national and four-time world champion martial artist turned pastor/author/coach and international speaker. Combining his fighting and faith, Joel discovered the secret for translating the psyche, skill set, and disciplines of a world-class fighter into every other facet of life, a system he calls: WIN*ology*.

Called a modern-day "warrior poet" with a deep love for mankind, Joel has dedicated his life to helping others learn to do the same and, subsequently, win in life at the highest levels.

Joel resides in North Texas with his wife and college sweetheart, Jennifer, and their daughters, Sydney and Blakely.

WANT MORE?

Check out all of Joel's other WIN*ology* products, keynote topics, and coaching products at:

www.joelscrivner.com

www.WINology.com

Joel is an expert coach, trainer, and public speaker and is sure to add just the right dynamic to your next corporate event.

Connect with Joel on Social Media

 Facebook.com/WINology

 Twitter.com/WINology101

 Instagram.com/JoelScrivner

 JoelScrivner.com/blog/

 Linkedin.com/pub/joel-scrivner/4b/985/151